Date Due

D1443304

Charter Your Boat for Profit

CHARTER YOUR BOAT
FOR PROFIT

By Fred Edwards

CORNELL MARITIME PRESS
Centreville, Maryland

Copyright © 1989 by Cornell Maritime Press, Inc.

Library of Congress Cataloging-in-Publication Data
Edwards, Fred.
      Charter your boat for profit / by Fred Edwards. — 1st ed.
      p.   cm.
      Includes bibliographical references.
      ISBN 0-87033-401-8:
      1. Boating industry. 2. Boats and boating—Chartering.
I. Title.
HD9993.B632E38   1989
387.5′42′068—dc20   89-43019
                              CIP

Manufactured in the United States of America
First edition

This book is dedicated to those who know what it means to stand a solitary watch. They have experienced the boredom, the fear, the exhaustion, the panic, the beauty, the awe, the responsibility—and the exhilaration. They have become gods for a while.

Contents

Appendices

Preface

IN what ways are people making money with boats today? When does a skipper need a captain's license? What does it take to get one? When must the boat be certified by the Coast Guard? How is it done? What is the real story about bareboat chartering? What is documentation and how do you do it? What responsibilities does an owner have toward the environment, the boat, captain, crew, passengers, and guests?

This book answers those questions and more. And it goes further by giving anyone who is interested in becoming a nautical entrepreneur a keen insight into the *business* of chartering: How do you start a charter business and get loans? What *must* you know about accounting, bookkeeping, and budgeting? What had you better know about marketing?

In order to find the answers, I sought out the experts and mailed nearly three hundred questionnaires to charter operators, and I personally contacted dozens of others in chartering and ancillary fields.

For the chapters involving the Coast Guard, I went to the Coast Guard itself. But I also obtained "second opinions" from civilians in the private sector who make their living interpreting and assisting others with the Coast Guard regulations. In like fashion, I received assistance from specialists in the fields of maritime liability, accounting, and marketing.

In all this, I have brought my own experience to bear—I am a Coast Guard–licensed captain and have taught for a national license prep organization. I have also documented my own boats, formed my own business entities, and created my own accounting and bookkeeping systems.

This fortunate combination of writer and experts has produced a book that boating entrepreneurs—beginners and old salts alike—should be happy to keep handy on their shelves, alongside *Dutton, Chapman*, the Rules of the Road, and the latest copies of their P&Ls and balance sheets.

I am grateful to the U.S. Coast Guard for its assistance with the technical parts of this book concerning Coast Guard regulations. The cooperation of the office of Rear Admiral John W. Kime, chief of the office of marine safety, security and environmental protection, was important in gaining the Coast Guard's position on the chartering business.

Particular thanks go to Lieutenant Commander Paul R. Von Protz—veteran of twenty-three years of service, with fourteen years in the Coast Guard's marine safety program—who reviewed the chapters on boat licenses, captain's licenses, inspected vessels, and bareboat chartering.

Thanks also go to Coast Guard Captain Thomas W. Boerger, commanding officer of the marine safety office in Tampa, who reviewed administrative law functions with me. And special thanks to Lieutenant Commander J. Pierce Guyer, who took time from his duties as the only investigating officer on Florida's west coast to review the chapter on administrative law.

Of equal importance has been the assistance of Captain Ron Wahl, founder of Sea School—The Law School of the Sea. Ron and the school's nationwide staff of Coast Guard licensing specialists helped interpret and translate those parts of the Code of Federal Regulations that apply to charter business owners and operators.

A special thank you goes to Linda D. Sylvia, P.A., an accountant and tax planning expert, whose help was instrumental in completion of the chapters on starting your business, obtaining a loan, and accounting and budgeting. Linda is an ACE (Active Core of Executives) member of SCORE, and she gave advice as she would with any SCORE client. She asks that I note that SCORE includes not only financial specialists but also executives in almost every field.

Thanks to Attorney Barry M. Snyder for his review and assistance with the chapter on liability. Snyder is a personal injury trial attorney in Miami, Florida, who holds a 100-ton master's license.

And a dip of the ensign to marketing consultant Frederick J. ("Fritz") Regner, Jr., president of Strategic Marketing, for his help with the chapters on marketing.

In order to make this book authentic, the author queried more than three hundred experts involved in or knowledgeable about the chartering business. Some have been quoted by name in the text, but the input from all who replied was vital to assimilating and presenting the chartering picture. A comprehensive list of these respondents appears in Appendix A.

Introduction

IT is essential that a charter operator or a person about to become one learn as much about the business as he can. However, until this book was published, there was no single volume like it that could adequately introduce the chartering business. That has all changed. This book either gives the facts or tells you where and how to get them.

Now you can find out what decisions you need to make, and how to make them. You can discover what the regulations demand, what the experts advise, and what experienced charter operators are saying.

Throughout this book, the term *charter operator* is used to describe a person in business, as opposed to a customer who charters a boat from him. Him? The male pronoun has been used as a concise way to refer to the men and women in the business.

And what does the book offer you if you already are a charter operator? It will help you to recapture ideas vital to your business that you might have bypassed earlier, and to confirm or alter key decisions you already have made.

The chapter on captain's licenses is designed for easy reference. It includes changes derived from the major overhaul of the Coast Guard's licensing system that was instituted by the Interim Final Rule effective December 1, 1987, and the Final Rule effective February 3, 1989.

If you are considering making money by chartering, you have a host of opportunities available. You might opt for a mom-and-pop live-aboard charter business. You might decide to turn your boat over to a chartering company. Perhaps you will join a chartering club. Or maybe you will elect to buy a yacht through a sale and lease-back agreement. The first two chapters are packed with dozens of similar options.

Here are some of the mechanics of this book:

• Why is the Coast Guard busy telling charter operators when they need licenses and when their boats need certificates of inspection? Because the Coast

Guard, under the Department of Transportation, is charged with administering and enforcing the regulations concerning—among other things—charter operations.

• The Coast Guard derives the bulk of its operating rules and regulations from the Code of Federal Regulations (CFR). Think of the CFR as coming from a computer that receives all the laws that Congress passes, sorts them into broad categories, and prints out each category as an operating manual. For example, Title 46, *Shipping*, comprises nine volumes. The first seven volumes constitute Chapter I of Title 46, which is: Coast Guard, Department of Transportation. (In this book, terms such as *Title 46, CFR Title 46, 46 CFR*, and *CFR 46* have the same meaning.)

• Although the Coast Guard's rules might appear to be disorganized, overlapping, and sometimes hopelessly bureaucratic, they *can* be subdivided into three functions. The Coast Guard refers to these functions as "trade, safety, and manning." In this book, those terms roughly translate to the topics of three of the chapters: boat licenses, inspected vessels, and captain's licenses, respectively.

• Sample forms used in the chartering business are not included because the book recommends that you obtain an attorney's advice about appropriate forms for your specific operation.

• The only references to income taxes are found in the chapter on starting your business. Major discussion of income taxes was not included for two reasons: (1) The tax laws change so swiftly that any information included would be quickly outdated; and (2) The book recommends that every charter operator use an accountant, who is paid to keep up to date on the tax laws.

• The terms *vessel, boat,* and *craft* are used interchangeably in an attempt to avoid monotony.

Of course, a single book cannot reproduce the volumes of federal regulations and the plethora of business acumen that it takes to be a successful enterpreneur. In fact, one of the chartering experts replied that a "primer" on how to run a charter business could be dangerous and irresponsible, because the inherent risk of boating increases as experience decreases. Although he declined to respond otherwise to the questionnaire, I thank him nonetheless for his idea. This book is indeed a "primer," in the sense that it was created to help each reader learn the *basics* of the charter business. It was created to teach you how to dog-paddle and how to don a life jacket before jumping into the water. Read it well. And good luck. See you on the water.

Charter Your Boat for Profit

CHAPTER 1

Making a Business of Boating

PSYCHOLOGISTS speak of water as the cradle of life. They hypothesize that humans seek the water because of a subconscious urge to return to some prehistoric life form in warm seas, or a drive to return to prenatal comfort in amniotic fluids. Those of us who simply like the water don't need all that theory. We merely accept the water's magical attraction, and return again and again, just as a compass needle always returns to north—because it has to.

What better way to be around the water than to mix business with pleasure and make boating a business? But isn't that a paradox? Can an entrepreneur turn boating into a business and still enjoy the water? He certainly can—as long as he understands and carries out the business of chartering as thoroughly as he practices the skills of seamanship and navigation.

As in any other business, a charter operator must go through the mechanics of getting started. And he will need upfront money, probably in the form of a loan. He ought to know enough basic accounting to find out where he is and where he's going. He will want the right kind of insurance coverage. And he should understand how to apply marketing principles to his business.

Unlike other businesses, a charter operator must be familiar with liabilities under maritime law. And he needs to know how the Coast Guard's role affects his charter business.

Like all businesses, there is no free ride, but success is possible.

One-Boat Charter Operations

In the Florida Keys, I met a couple who were completing two weeks on their 28-foot sloop with a second couple who had chartered the boat. It had been the latter couple's first exposure to sailing. The inside of the boat was steamy from the May heat of southern Florida, and it was smelly and dirty from two weeks of gunkholing. But those four sailors (the charter party had become sailors too) seemed to be completing the happiest two weeks of their lives.

The captain told me privately that he and his wife accepted only charter parties they felt certain would be compatible with their laid-back lifestyle. Another two-week charter party was waiting to board as soon as his debarking friends showered in the marina and he took them to the airport to fly north. Now *that's* a mom-and-pop charter operation!

In a somewhat more elegant setting are Jeff and Terri Siben, who live aboard their 1912 John Trumpy design motor yacht *Ibis*. Two years`of refurbishing the 70-foot wooden vessel made her a cosmetic contemporary of the former presidential yacht *Sequoia*, in her finest hour. The Sibens specialize in taking corporate groups for sunset cruises at $1,000 a cruise, plus optional (catered) food and entertainment.

The Sibens' charter business gives them enough return to spend summers in Newport, Rhode Island, and Oakdale, Long Island; and winters in Fort Lauderdale, Florida. Jeff says that although he definitely won't get rich, he pays all his expenses and eats lobsters and shrimp.[1]

Once in a while, an operator welcomes aboard a charter party that he will remember the rest of his life. Les Lathrop, who has lived most of his forty-two years aboard a gaff-rigged Bahamian ketch named *Ask No Quarter*, is no stranger to prominent and exotic guests. The third volume of his boat's guest log contains thirty-eight pages of entries by more than four hundred visitors from England, Tunisia, Turks & Caicos, Japan, Australia, the Bahamas, and the United States.

But the most memorable entry reads: "Charles and party. A beautiful day and a most enjoyable time." This came from the day Les took Great Britain's Prince Charles and a party of eight out for scuba diving, snorkeling, and trolling off Eleuthera, in the Bahamas.

Les, now a dockmaster and yacht-club cruise director in the United States, says, "I'd quit my job to have another day with him. He was a very neat guy to be around. After he signed the log, he told me that he had never had so much fun doing so many things in so little time."

Of course an owner doesn't have to live aboard his boat to charter it out. And he doesn't have to take out royalty. If he meets the Coast Guard regulations (see chapters on boat and captain's licenses, inspected vessels, administrative law, and bareboat chartering for pleasure), he can charter out his yacht with a captain or as a bareboat. He can charter it to almost anybody. And he can live afloat or ashore.

Fleet Charter Operations

A large yacht-charter operation often carries out two functions—yacht management for owners and the operation of a yacht-charter business. The functions often overlap. Maintenance, for example, is done for both owners and customers. This section will discuss the charter operator aspect, using information received during a telephone interview with Frank Jordan, president of Virgin Islands Power Yacht Charters (VIP Yachts) in St. Thomas. (See chapter on yacht management for information on turning your boat over to others.)

VIP Yachts has been in business in the Virgin Islands since 1984. There are more than six hundred charterboats in its area of operations, and fewer than fifty of them are powerboats. Twenty-three of those, from 38 to 66 feet in length, belong to VIP.

Jordan says, "We think that motor yacht chartering is a nice way to do business, although it's very complicated and time-consuming. Renting out a condominium, putting it on the water, and adding a diesel engine requires a lot of imagination. But it's more fun dealing with luxury yachts in the Caribbean than making widgets in New Hampshire."

Jordan offers the following advice for those who would like to start a charter operation in the Virgins:

1. Economy of scale. In the Virgins, the mom-and-pop charter business has gone the way of the mom-and-pop grocery store. Don't start without ten boats. It is most difficult when your inventory is two to seven boats, because, to meet your competition, you still need an advertising budget suited for a minimum of ten boats. This means $50,000 to $100,000 a year. And you must plan for a continuing capital investment for the first two years.

2. Insurance. The ability to get insurance can be critical. An insurance company might expect a new charter operator to have experience. How does he have that if he's just starting?

3. Local knowledge. A person considering bringing investment funds to the Virgins must understand the elements that are unique there, such as dockage, regulations, and the lead times necessary for accomplishing tasks.

4. Employees. It can take time to hire qualified personnel, because you must compete for employees. You might have to stay in business two years to show permanency before a competent employee is likely to leave another job and work for you.

5. Maintenance. The most critical requirement is to have enough working capital for preventive maintenance. A new charter operator should have sufficient capital for a complete inventory of spare parts, particularly for powerboats.

Jordan added that the five points of advice also apply to other localities, such as the Bahamas and Belize, where problems can be even more complex because of foreign governments.

Boating Instruction

Offering instructions is an ego-rewarding way to help defray boating expenses. Thousands of skippers use their boats to teach daysailing and cruising. A skipper/owner can tailor the instruction to each student's level of knowledge and abilities, and can arrange the schedule to fit that of the student.

An entrepreneur might want to expand and establish a school. A school may have a fleet of boats, or flotillas of different kinds of boats. Programs can include daysailing, offshore cruises, and even ocean passages. A school often offers a certification of the graduate's qualifications as a charterer, or a guarantee of a free course if a graduate is refused a charter.

Although the raison d'être of a school is instruction, this doesn't prevent a school from also chartering out its boats. Much depends upon the operator's position in the market. (For discussion of a marketing position, see chapter on the marketing plan.) For example, Paul Fenn, president of Coastline Sailing School and Yacht Charters in Noank, Connecticut, stated that in 1987 his company split about 50-50 between instruction and chartering. On the other hand, Ned McMahon, operations manager of Steve Colgate's Offshore Sailing School in New York, reported that 99 percent of his business was instruction.

What special attraction draws clients to sailing schools? Location ranks high on the list. McMahon of Colgate's says, "Quality instruction at the best locations." Fenn of Coastline says, "Located just south of Newport, Rhode Island, we have a superb location for both daysailing as well as cruising. Being able to offer both charterers and cruising students the opportunity to sail to such ports as Block Island, Newport, Shelter Island, and Montauk Point is a big selling point for us." He adds that being a member of the American Sailing Association helps the school a great deal.

Suzanne Pogell, president of Womanship in Annapolis, Maryland, found a marketing position that could include 50 percent of the student population. Her program specializes in women teaching sailing to women. Her approach is that "nobody yells." Cashing in on the recently booming powerboat market, Pogell has started a similar program for powerboat instruction.

Powerboat instruction has also been added to at least one branch of the International School of Sailing. Its course is advertised as a five-day live-aboard "Powerboat Skipper's School," operating out of Fort Lauderdale.

Saltwater Sportfishing

Many sportfishing charter operators say that, if you like to fish, this is the only way to go. Radio broadcaster Mel Berman, who hosts an hour-long outdoors-oriented program on Saturday mornings, says:

> At first I had no intention of running charters. It just turned out that when I got this boat, I thought it would be fun to meet different people, and help defray a lot of the cost. It turns out that it worked very well for me by giving me the ability to promote my charters on my radio program, and improve my opportunities to a great extent.

Berman, who has a six-pack license (so named because it authorizes the holder to take six or fewer passengers for hire on certain vessels), takes his 34-foot Delta, *Mel-Fin 3,* out for Spanish and king mackerel, and for grouper.

Is there money in sportfishing? You bet your bimini. *Motor Boating & Sailing* writer Sid Stapleton listed an annual balance sheet for Jim Courbier, owner/captain of a 45-foot Hatteras, that shows a pretax profit of $42,000. And, after taking depreciation, his *taxable income* was $7,000. All of that is the gravy on top of entering (and winning) fishing tournaments in the Bahamas. It's not a bad way to pay your boat payments and expenses.[2]

Head Boats and Party Boats

A head boat charges so much a person (a "head") to take scheduled fishing trips, while a party boat generally contracts for a group. The same boat may be used for both purposes. Charter operators for these boats normally are prepared to provide fishing gear and bait, and often will even bait the hooks—as well as clean the fish!

Schedules can be tight, and electronic fishfinder gear often is necessary to beat the competition: The operator who gets the fish gets the customers.

Does a head-boat or party-boat owner have time to fish? When asked if *he* fished for pleasure, Captain Wilson M. Hubbard, who operates three boats in the Gulf of Mexico, simply reported, "Not enough." However, Hubbard may have let entrepreneurship rearrange his priorities, as he has added an excursion sailboat, a boardwalk restaurant, and ten boardwalk shops to his charter business.

Lake and Stream Fishing

The hinterland is full of charter operators who know that you don't have to live around salt water to enjoy some of the greatest fishing in the country. You can go for freshwater fish, letting the charterers subsidize it. And the subsidy can be good.

Fred C. Edwards (my son), a Kansas City, Missouri, fisherman, reports that bass guides on nearby Truman Lake are earning $125 per day, plus gas and food. A half day runs $75.

The fees go up as you go down to Lake Okeechobee, Florida. Captain Terry Arnold, who teaches captain's license prep courses there, reports bass-guide rates in season at $200 per day, and out of season at $185. He was impressed with some fancy bass boats and pickup trucks belonging to charter operators along the north rim of the lake.

Dive Boats

Operating a dive boat is as specialized as scuba diving itself. Every dive-shop operator and dive-boat skipper who responded to my questionnaire stated that the captain should be a certified diver, and preferably an advanced diver.

A dive-boat skipper does more than take passengers to a dive site and say, "Here it is." He helps fill and inspect air tanks, and he checks their level before repetitive dives. He needs to be sure the dives are planned and carried out in a manner that will avert decompression sickness ("the bends"). If he has another licensed captain aboard, he might do double duty as divemaster or instructor. (See chapter on captain's licenses.)

The skipper also gives myriad special diving instructions to each group he takes out. Jon Hardy, owner of Argo Diving Services on Catalina Island, California, says that his special rules are "too long to list, but they cover entries, exits, depths, equipment used, staying with a guide, buddy diving signals," and many more.

Since all of these special requirements are routine to certified divers, the dive-boat business is ideal for a person who loves to dive. For example, when Ron and Libby Burch, owners of Treasure Island Divers, Inc., in Treasure Island, Florida, have a day off, they take their 20-foot Wellcraft back out into the Gulf of Mexico and go diving.

Diving is a self-regulated industry, whereby certification agencies train divers—in the classroom and under water—to increasing levels of competence. A diver can't even get his tank filled at an authorized station unless he has earned a basic certification card (C-card) from a recognized agency.

An entrepreneur considering taking certification courses should be sure to affiliate with an agency that receives reciprocal recognition from the major agencies. (Appendix D provides a partial list of certification agencies.)

Certification levels for the agencies are roughly parallel, with four or five steps required to reach either the master (recreational) level or the professional level (which allows the holder to instruct at an agency-authorized facility).

Diving is big business. A charter operator who affiliates with a certification agency can climb aboard a market that's up and planing. He can give classes at his dive shop and on his boat, sell his students diving gear, take them back out on the boat for recreational dives, re-enroll them in advanced classes, and then start all over.

The agencies can provide administrative support, including classroom supplies, publicity materials, and a mail-order inventory of merchandise; some even offer insurance. At least one agency, the Professional Association of Diving Instructors (PADI), offers a book on how to establish and run a dive-shop business.[3]

Water Skiing

Duke Cullimore, public relations director for the American Water Ski Association (AWSA), explains that there are two types of boats for water-ski chartering—boats made specifically for water skiing, and general recreational runabouts.

He notes that relatively few of the former are in charter service because their specific nature makes them suited only to accomplished water skiers. Because such skiers often have their own personal equipment, a charter operator probably would furnish only the boat. Untutored water skiers seeking experience behind these specialized boats usually would attend a school where they would be towed behind boats belonging to the school and operated by skilled school staff.

Cullimore continues:

For general recreational boats for rent for water skiing, the operator would need several pairs of combination skis in various sizes, a 75-foot tow rope fitted with a handle, and some U.S. Coast Guard Type III personal flotation devices in various sizes. The towboat should be fitted with a large, wide-angle rear-view mirror that the driver can use to watch the skier. For safety purposes, the rental operator should insist on an observer being aboard the towboat in addition to the driver. Also, the rental operator should have on hand copies of the AWSA *Guide to Safe Water Skiing,* which explains towboat operation when pulling a skier, skier and driver communication, and much additional safety information.

Houseboats

A big lake or a winding river can provide an excellent opportunity for an entrepreneur to get into houseboat chartering. A 40-foot-by-14-foot houseboat on calm waters can offer a relaxing, pleasurable week to many families who would never consider trying a sailboat or a trawler. Houseboats are floating cottages, with something for everybody: fishing; snorkeling or scuba diving from the stern; sunbathing on the top deck; relaxing in the lounge; and exploring the water wilderness—with range, refrigerator, dishes, and linens aboard.

Billy Miller, manager of Miller's Suwannee Houseboats, in Suwannee, Florida, expresses surprise at the large rental response: "We have a large number of customers from inside Florida as well as a large number from out of the state."

Regardless of the relative luxury of a houseboat, Miller says that the Suwannee might not suit everybody, "because it's not commercialized. There are no towns to step off at. It's a wild and natural river."

Excursion Boats

People will pay to go on the water to look and dance and eat and drink. They go out to watch whales, to observe rocket launches and sunsets, and to see sailboats race. They climb aboard paddle-wheel boats to take harbor cruises, bay cruises, river cruises, and lake cruises. And they go out in glass-bottomed boats to gaze at fish, coral, and scuba divers.

An excursion boat can be of any size and for any purpose. I once saw a three-masted sailing vessel, crewed by fully costumed pirates, carrying sightseers around the bay. One pirate was swinging through the rigging, brandishing a flashing scimitar. The passengers loved it!

Ferryboats

Ferryboats also come in all configurations, from rowboats used to carry pedestrians across narrow waterways, to large vehicle-carrying ferryboats with propellers at both ends, from train-carrying vessels that have transited the English Channel, to state-of-the-art air-cushion vessels.

Wherever people want to cross over water to reach land, there can be a market for a ferry service. Consider this example, extracted from information provided by Catalina Express, which operates a fleet of four fast ferryboats between San Pedro, California, and Catalina Island:

> In July of 1981, Catalina Channel Express was started by Doug Bombard, Greg Bombard, and Tom Rutter with one fifty-five-passenger boat. These men were born and raised on Catalina Island. Beginning as a commuter service for islanders wishing a longer day off the island, the company steadily grew from the first day of operation and has expanded into the tourist industry . . . The Catalina Express has proudly served more than 600,000 passengers to Catalina Island.

Recreational Boats

There's room for recreational boats wherever you find water: Hobie Cats, water bikes, iceboats, canoes, rafts, paddleboats, and even inner tubes. Each has a place in the charter business, because when people get near water, they want to get on it and in it.

Airboats

What a perfect adaptation for swamps and shallow grassy lakes! Take a shallow-draft hull, maybe a pair of pontoons, mount a radial engine and propeller above the stern, and fly across the water. Take along some sightseers to pay the overhead. Then take a day off and roar out to get some fish, frogs, or game.

Except for the engine, there is little maintenance. And out-of-water stowage is quite simple, since there is no keel that requires the craft to be placed up on blocks. In fact, some operators trailer their airboats from site to site and leave them on the trailers when they are not in use. On the other hand, a fleet operator might just leave his boats in his backyard between charters.

Submarines

Charter submarines became a reality when the Coast Guard certified *Atlantis III* for forty-seven passengers in 1987. The 65-foot craft, built by Sub-Aquatics Development Corporation, is operating in the Virgin Islands. Builders are currently scheduling another submarine for the Virgins, as well as submersibles for Hawaii, Guam, and the Florida Keys.

Restaurants

Want to open a fast-food restaurant on the beach, but can't get through the local zoning boards? One operator decided simply to float a hamburger stand up to the seaward edge of a swimming beach. It's not as easy as it sounds, however, because most communities retain jurisdiction for sanitation enforcement even over floating restaurants. And either the community or the Coast Guard will oversee vessel safety regulations. But the opportunity is there.

Another operator attempted to move a barge into the Dry Tortugas, seven tiny coral islets located seventy miles west of Key West. Moored at a place where not even fresh water is available, he would be able to sell food, drinks, ice, fuel, spare parts, batteries, fishing tackle, bait, medical supplies, snorkel and scuba gear, and, yes, water. So far, the National Park Service administration refuses to consider it.

Then there's the five-star cruising restaurant *U.S. Bon Appetit*, co-owned by Austrian restaurateur Peter Kreuziger. The vessel is a sixty-seven-ton steel trawler, powered by a Detroit 871 diesel. Although it can embark up to forty-seven diners from its berth in Dunedin, Florida, it often gets underway with only an intimate table for two, a chef, stewards . . . and a violinist. Captain "K," as he is called, charges $250 an hour, with a three-hour minimum for larger parties. Costs for smaller parties are discreetly negotiable.

Or what about a restaurant and casino? *Soundings* magazine reported in 1987 that entrepreneur John Alvin Davis III was considering buying inactive oil rigs and converting them into offshore casinos that would be serviced by ferries and launches.

In the same article, David Robinson, of Floating Structures, Inc., in New York, which represents Consafe Singapore, envisioned a two-hundred-room resort—with restaurants, tennis courts, and marina—to be anchored on Australia's Great Barrier Reef.[4]

Sign Boats

Bob and Sally are strolling along the beach one evening when a message forms and flashes toward shore: "Sally—marry me—Bob." During their honeymoon, a boat just beyond the swimming area pops up a sign: "Tacos—All you can eat—$4.95—The Beach House—South End of Beach." As with floating restaurants, an entrepreneur thinking of launching a sign boat should check with shoreside authorities to see if he falls under their jurisdiction. In this case, it might mean conforming to local sign regulations.

Television and Films

Rick Smith, owner of Pisces Divers in Miami Beach, reports that his fleet of dive boats has become well known to camera crews. His 48-footer has been used to film two episodes of "Miami Vice," and it was used to film four movies and a soap opera. The boat has also been used in a number of national and international commercials for soap, coffee, and cigarettes. As a dive boat equipped for film crews, it was a logical platform from which to film re-created wreck sites for the Children's Television Workshop in New York.

Ralph T. Heath, Jr., director of the Suncoast Seabird Sanctuary, Inc., in Indian Shores, Florida, said that his 24-foot boat is permanently configured for camera crews. It is adapted for a special IMAX (for wide screens) camera, which was used for coverage for the Smithsonian Institution and the 1985 World's Fair in Japan. Other projects have included "You Asked For It," "20/20," and "tons and tons" of commercials and other film.

Heath, whose sanctuary is internationally prominent among environmentalists and lovers of wildlife, says that media representatives contact him almost daily about using his boat. He warns, however, that such interest doesn't happen overnight, and that a charter operator should not attempt to go into business solely for television filming. He says, "Don't set up your boat for a camera crew and wait for someone to call on the telephone, unless you're extremely well known."

The Final Report Card

Charter operators everywhere report that they get their share of customers who just do not understand boats. Bill Sheriff, owner/manager of Briarwood on Lake Taneycomo, in Branson, Missouri, was surprised to find charterers who considered his 14-foot aluminum vee-hulled boats with 18-horsepower outboards to be toys.

Charter operators also report uniformly that maintenance is crucial to having a boat ready for a customer at a given time and place.

Margot Wilson, office manager of Pacific Quest Charters in Vancouver (Canada), states:

> We have done everything from flying a repairman in to fix the problem to delivering a boat to the distressed party so they can continue on their way with the least amount of difficulty. If the problem isn't too serious, then we ask the charterer to have it fixed and we reimburse them for the repair and their trouble.

Penny Spencer, co-owner of Eleuthera-Bahamas-Charters says, "We maintain well for our charter customers, because we owe it to them. However, boats break down. People who charter a lot realize this. But if they are not used to chartering a lot, something like a broken fan belt can be disappointing."

Penny's business partner, John Spencer, reports that they, like most charter companies, keep a chase boat on call, and they depend upon radio and local assistance if a chartered boat gets too far away for immediate assistance from the home base.

Bill Allgaier, president of Bay Breeze Yacht Charters in Traverse City, Michigan, notes that, in addition to the chase boat, "We are on call twenty-four hours to ensure that all breakdowns are handled promptly."

And for a fifth comment, how can you beat this for a problem? Ken Maxwell, booking agent for BVI Bareboats in the British Virgins, relates the following: "A charterer radioed for assistance because his boat was being held by a 'magnetic force.' The rescue crew found that he had forgotten to raise his second anchor!"

Put it all together, and that's what making a business of boating is all about. Operators of every type of charter boat have reported that their businesses are fun but exacting. As VIP's Frank Jordan says, "It's better than making widgets."

They all stress that a charter operator has to exercise every consideration that applies to other businesses, while paying close attention to the requirements peculiar to chartering. (Those considerations and requirements, which were listed briefly at the beginning of this chapter, are the subjects of succeeding chapters.)

Summary

1. People who like being around the water, and who want to be in business, can make a business of boating.

2. To ensure success, a chartering business must be run as exactingly as any other business.

3. Maintenance can be the lifeblood of chartering.

CHAPTER 2

Yacht Management

THERE are four basic ways you can put a boat into charter service without running the entire business yourself:

1. Turn the boat over to a charter organization or broker;
2. Buy a boat through a turnkey plan;
3. Join a chartering club; or
4. Let a captain do it.

Let's examine each of these in detail.

Turn the Boat Over to a Charter Organization or Broker

In general, a charter organization operates, maintains, and charters out boats for the owners, while a broker simply finds customers for the boats included on his listing. Each entity is sometimes called an agent, because in fact each *is* an agent for the owner.

Although some large charter organizations use only boats sold through them (see following section on turnkey plans), many charter companies are looking for boats to add to their fleets. You might find such a company near home, or, if your local season is short, you could benefit by seeking one in a warmer climate—even as far away as the Virgin Islands.

Turning over your boat to a charter organization is like converting it to a time-share condominium. The manager advertises the entire condominium, maintains the complex, and rents out the rooms. He charges each owner for his share of the maintenance and gives him a percentage of the rent collected.

Charter-company contracts can vary, depending upon the boat owner's wishes and the organization he selects. The owner might offer his boat as a bareboat or a crewed boat (see chapter on bareboat chartering). If it is crewed, he might be the captain, or the organization might provide a captain. The owner might keep the boat at his dock, or the charter organization might provide a dock. In short, by finding the right organization, the owner can place his boat out for charter in a way that will suit his exact needs.

How do you find the right organization? Captain Dan, owner/manager of Dolphin Landings Charter Boat Center in Florida, offers the following guidelines for finding a local organization:

1. Look in the Yellow Pages to find established companies;
2. Select a company capable of handling your type of boat;
3. Check out the track record of that company by contacting customers who have chartered through it; and
4. Work out a contract that is agreeable to you and the company.

The same principles apply to finding a charter organization away from home. Instead of using the Yellow Pages, you might check out ads in national boating magazines. And it is a good idea to contact owners whose boats have been handled by the organization. You can gain vital information about a company's attitude toward maintenance and public relations just by chartering a boat from it.

An important marriage of the chartering and broker functions is found in Charlotte Amalie, St. Thomas, Virgin Islands, where a nonprofit association called The Virgin Islands Charteryacht League (VICL) sets standards for crewed charters. Each member boat must have a licensed captain, commercial documentation, and a minimum of $300,000 liability insurance. Membership in the VICL, coupled with membership in a St. Thomas brokers' clearinghouse, has been the solution for more than 175 yachts.

If you elect to list your boat with a broker, you will probably be expected to insure and maintain the boat, and set the charter fee, and the broker will obtain customers in exchange for a percentage of the fees.

Should the broker be local? The key here is that he should know the boat in order to market it the most effectively. If you are going to place a fleet of sister ships in the Caribbean, a broker from anywhere in the United States or Canada might travel there once a season to see the boats. If you have a single boat, it could be a different story. Louise S. Dailey, president of Jubilee Yacht Charters in Darien, Connecticut, advises that it is often best to list a single boat with a local broker who can see the boat. Then, if a broker from another area has a customer for that type of boat in your area, he will call local brokers for their listings.

Buy a Boat through a Turnkey Plan

A "turnkey plan" refers to a business deal whereby a company sells a boat and contracts to charter it out for the owner. Each company might use a different name for its program, and programs can vary immensely, as will be shown.

In the past, turnkey plans were widely used as tax loopholes, but they should be regarded as business propositions under the current laws. A turnkey plan can help you invest in a boat, or buy one, through cash flow as well as depreciation, while making the vessel available to you for your occasional use. Such a plan is generally suitable for a boat costing more than $100,000. If this idea interests you, start by comparing current turnkey plans from companies that offer them (see ads in major boating magazines), and discuss the plans with your accountant.

Here are simplified examples[1] of five plans offered:

1. The owner pays mortgage, insurance, taxes, registration, licenses, and 50 percent of costs of expensive repairs and parts (amount stated in contract). The company pays all other expenses, plus 50 percent of costs of expensive repairs and parts, and forwards the owner 50 percent of gross charter revenues.

2. The owner pays only the mortgage. The company pays all other costs and forwards the owner an agreed-upon, fixed percentage of the boat's purchase value each month—at least enough to cover the mortgage payment.

3. The owner pays everything: mortgage, insurance, taxes, registration, licenses, all maintenance and repairs, and a share of the company's monthly overhead. The company forwards the owner 60 percent of gross charter revenues.

4. The owner pays everything. The company forwards 80 percent of gross charter revenues, less advertising costs and outside commissions, with a guarantee of a minimum net income after expenses (but excluding mortgage payments).

5. Sale and long-term lease-back. The owner pays nothing during the term of the lease and receives no cash.

Most plans include a commission to the owner for referrals and owner-generated charters. Some plans allow for termination with two- to six-month notification. Some provide for refurbishment at the end of the charter period, at additional cost.

Each turnkey plan includes provisions for the owner to use the boat a certain number of weeks each year. This accommodates an owner who might normally use his boat for that number of weeks anyway, and leave it languishing without income at the local yacht club or marina for the rest of the year.

The plans outlined are geared for loans of 80 percent of the purchase price. Depending upon the plan, qualifying parameters run as follows:

• Minimum net worth equal to from one to two times the purchase price;
• Minimum liquid assets equal to the 20 percent down payment, or up to 15 or 20 percent of the loan; and
• Total debt not to be in excess of two and a half to three times the buyer's annual income.

The Bottom Line for Turnkey Plans

As can be seen, if you are considering a turnkey plan, you must work carefully with your accountant to find the plan best suited to your financial situation and goals. Be sure you intend to use your "owner time" because you like boats, not just because it's available each year. Test the boat, or a boat like it, before buying, to see if it's one you would like to charter. And you should charter with the management firm before buying, to get a charterer's impression of the firm's attitude and competence. Finally, you should be fully satisfied that the company you select has a track record; can handle maintenance; and has the financial capability to fulfill the contract promises.

Join a Chartering Club

A chartering club offers a splendid market of captive customers, simply because people without boats have joined in order to charter from that club. Why would they do that? Because a club can attract charter parties by organizing group events. *And* because chartering clubs advertise rates considerably lower than straight charter rates.

Rates might be lower because the club does not dock or maintain the boats, or because the club receives initiation fees and annual dues. Chartering clubs offer a viable way of putting a boat up for charter, and they can earn certain benefits for the owner.

The following description of a chartering club was prepared from information obtained during a telephone interview with Howard Huntsberry of Florida Sailing Charter Club, in Coconut Grove, Florida.

• A boat owner pays the initiation fee, but is exempted from the annual dues (currently $200). The club sets the charter fee, based upon the boat's size. The club advertises the boat through its newsletter and other outlets.

• A potential charter party must be a club member, and be certified for minimum proficiency through the American Sailing Association (ASA). (The ASA relationship also allows for group insurance rates.)

• Regardless of the charterer's certification, if the boat is over 30 feet long, the owner has the option of refusing him after a checkout.

• The owner receives 95 percent of all charter fees.

Not all of Huntsberry's customers will have to go to Florida to charter boats. He plans to open new clubs in Atlanta and Chicago, so that members (including boat owners) can sail in the North in summer and in the South in winter. He also is developing reciprocity with existing clubs on the Pacific Coast, and is negotiating for the same in the Bahamas and the Virgins.

Let a Captain Do It

On the island of Cozumel, Mexico, I met a professional captain who lived aboard a 38-foot sloop that was kept in Bristol fashion. He had been hired to maintain the boat and to take out charter parties that originated through the owner's business in Texas. The captain was allowed to drum up his own charters from American tourists visiting the island. Every month or so, the owner would fly to Cozumel for a weekend of sailing and diving—and to inspect his boat and pay the captain his nominal wage.

No matter where it takes place, a charter operation like that needs two elements for success: (1) The *right* captain, one who understands what the owner wants and will do it; and (2) a contract and insurance, obtained with the help of an attorney and an insurance agent.

To find a captain, first look for strong credentials—a captain's license from the Coast Guard; a substantiated, verifiable track record; and credible references. Then be sure you are entirely comfortable with his or her personality. Finally, come to grips with how much autonomy and use of your funds he needs to charter out your boat for you, and how much you are willing to give. At that stage, you are ready to strike a financial deal, seal it with a contract, and protect your investment with insurance.

Summary

1. A charter organization can operate and maintain your boat, and obtain customers. A charter broker can find customers.

2. A turnkey plan can be an excellent choice for certain boat buyers or investors who are prepared to buy boats with prices above $100,000.

3. A chartering club is an easy, sociable way to put a boat up for charter.

4. Choosing a captain to charter out your boat for you is like paying a partner to prospect for gold in your absence.

CHAPTER 3

Starting Your Business

PERHAPS you are a pleasure-boat skipper who has been paying through the nose for your hobby—loan payments, slip fees, insurance premiums, maintenance costs, haul-out charges, you name it. Your boat is the traditional hole-in-the-water into which you throw money. You figure that any cash you can earn by converting to chartering will help pay some of those bills.

Or maybe you are an entrepreneur planning to go into chartering strictly on a business basis. For you it's a sophisticated game that allows you to use venture capital and cash flow to build a fleet. You expect to maximize profits and minimize losses, and move on to another business.

Whether you match either of these two types, or fall somewhere in between, heed the words of Linda D. Sylvia, P.A., an accounting and tax-planning expert for twelve years. She says:

> The first thing you should do is ask yourself whether you have the ability and natural fortitude to start a small business. Being in business is a twenty-four-hour-a-day job, seven days a week. You might work only so many hours at the office or on the boat, but you definitely will wake up in the middle of the night, thinking, "Oh, I should have done this," or "Tomorrow I should do that."

The majority of small businesses fail during the first year, but even first-year survival doesn't ensure success. Accountant Sylvia says that for most service businesses it takes five years before you are very comfortable that you are going to have a successful enterprise. She explained that, with a chartering business, you might do it in less time if you have a market, and if you persevere.

Frank Jordan, president of Virgin Islands Power Yacht Charters in St. Thomas, describes the charter business this way: "People will fail if they think it's a romantic business; it's a seven-day-a-week operation, and the business

22

better be good. You can't pass on mistakes, but must swallow them. This means you must have good accounting and cost control. You need a good local CPA to guide you through from the beginning."

Below are ten questions[1] the Small Business Administration (SBA) offers to help you decide whether you are the kind of person who can start a business and make it go:

1. Are you a self-starter who does things on your own, without being told to get going?

2. Do you like other people and get along with just about anybody?

3. Can you lead others by getting most people to go along when you start something?

4. Do you assume responsibility because you like to take charge of things and see them through?

5. Are you a good organizer who likes to have a plan before starting, and who usually gets things lined up when a group wants to do something?

6. Are you a good worker who keeps going as long as necessary, and who doesn't mind working hard for something you want?

7. When it's time for a decision, can you make up your mind in a hurry if you have to, and expect your decision usually to turn out all right?

8. Can people trust what you say, because you only say things you mean?

9. If you make up your mind to do something, do you stick with it and let nothing stop you?

10. Is your health such that you never run down?

The SBA says that if you answered yes to most of the questions, you probably have what it takes to run a business. If not, you are likely to have more trouble than you can handle by yourself.

It Takes More than Ability

A skipper who reads the ten questions just listed might say, "Nothing new there. If I couldn't answer yes to those questions, I'd never survive as a captain." However, surviving in business demands certain skills beyond those needed offshore in a storm. Here's what the SBA says:

The basic survival skills include a working knowledge of basic recordkeeping; financial management; personnel management; market analysis; breakeven analysis; product or service knowledge; federal, state and local tax knowledge; legal structures; and communication skills.[2]

Your Three Best Friends

The key words from the preceding sentence are "a working knowledge." Once a charter operator acquires a working knowledge of business skills, he can rely upon experts for assistance with the details. Linda Sylvia says, "If you are going into business, your three best friends are your accountant, your commercial lender, and your attorney." There is a good way to get one of each at no charge.

Unless Congress has tossed the Small Business Administration over the side—and the Service Corps of Retired Executives (SCORE) along with it—call the nearest SCORE chapter. SCORE is a nationwide group of more than 12,000 volunteers in 592 offices who volunteer their time to assist people with small businesses at no charge. SCORE chapter president Lester M. Unger says, "Even if SCORE is removed from the SBA, the Department of Commerce might take it over. If that should not take place, SCORE will probably remain in some form, because it is cost free."

Alternatively, if you decide to hire an accountant or an attorney, shop around by word of mouth, just as you do when you're buying a new boat. All other choices being equal, you might find one who offers the first hour free. That will give you a good test, because if you can't prepare and state your case clearly in an hour, as sure as the tide rises and falls you don't have a handle on how you are going to run the business.

If the person you select *does* charge for the first session, and he's reputable, he is not likely to claim-jump you while you're prospecting. He'll earn bigger fees after you've found the mother lode and need more involved assistance— and can afford to pay more. He—like you—is in business, and knows the basic precept of customer loyalty: "Let your customer leave smiling, and he'll come back."

Here's the bottom line. If you carefully develop a business plan with an accountant and an attorney, and stick with it on your own, your return visits will be few and short.[3]

After developing your business plan, take it to a marine lender, or a commercial loan officer—perhaps a vice president—at the bank. This is the chance to say, "I'm not asking for a loan, but would like you to know what I'm going to do. Here's my plan. What do you think?" That ought to bring your third friend on board, so you can turn to him when you *do* need a loan. Now let's get down to the nitty-gritty.

Your Business Entity

Evaluate your planned business with the accountant and the attorney to determine the best entity for your charter operation. Reevaluate as the operation grows, and as the tax laws change. Here are basic descriptions of the various business entities:

Sole Proprietor

This is the simplest business structure to set up and operate. The only requirements are that the charter operator be self-employed and the sole owner, and that the business not be incorporated. Except for obtaining a fictitious name (if the business will use one; more on this shortly), he simply obtains the necessary licenses (to be discussed) and sets up shop.

The major advantage of a sole proprietorship is full control over the running of the business. A major disadvantage is that the sole proprietor is personally liable for debts incurred by the proprietorship. Thus, his personal assets can be taken to pay business debts. Other disadvantages are that the proprietor must provide all contributions of capital, labor, and skill; and that the proprietorship has limited life.

A charter operator who is a sole proprietor may be eligible to participate in a Keogh (HR-10) plan or an Individual Retirement Arrangement (IRA).

At federal income tax time, a sole proprietor fills out Schedule C, showing income and expenses, and adds it to his return.

Partnership

Two or more individuals can join together in a partnership. By so doing, they reap the advantage of pooling capital, or skills and labor, or both. Net profits go to the partners in agreed-upon proportions.

A partnership has the following disadvantages:

1. Unlimited liability: Each partner's personal assets can be taken to pay business debts incurred by any partner;
2. Loss of full control by one or more partners;
3. Difficulty in transferring a partnership interest; and
4. Limited life.

The partnership agreement can be written or verbal. In fact, the IRS says:

> If you and another person decide to share profits and losses from a business, and each of you contributes cash, other property, labor, or skill to the business, there is usually a partnership, whether or not you make a formal partnership agreement.[4]

A husband and wife are included in the preceding definition of a partnership. However, the IRS says that family members will only be recognized as partners if one of the following two requirements[5] is met:

> 1. If capital is a material income-producing factor, they must acquire their capital interest in a bona fide transaction (even if by gift or purchase from another family member), actually own the partnership interest, and actually have control over the interest. A capital interest in a partnership means an interest in the partnership's assets that is distributable to a partner upon the withdrawal of that partner from the partnership or upon the liquidation of the partnership. The mere right to share in the earnings and profits is not a capital interest.
> 2. If capital is not a material income-producing factor, they must contribute substantial or vital services to the partnership.

The IRS will *not* accept a joint undertaking merely to share expenses as a partnership.

Normally, a working member's share of the partnership income will be taxable for Social Security purposes. And he may be eligible for the same retirement plans available to sole proprietors.

A partnership prepares IRS Form 1065 for information and sends it to the IRS. Using Form 1065, it prepares a Schedule K-1 for each partner, showing his share of profits and losses. Each partner then transfers the amounts from his Schedule K-1 to appropriate lines of his income tax return, and keeps the Schedule K-1 with his records.

Corporation

This type of business structure is called a "C corporation," to distinguish it from an "S corporation."

Accountant Linda Sylvia says, "A corporation is the greatest thing since Santa Claus. Think of all the kids running around believing in an invisible person called Santa Claus. Then think of all the adults running around believing in an invisible person called a corporation."

A corporation is indeed an artificial person, created by a state government to engage in business. Its advantages include:

1. Limited liability for shareholders;
2. Ability to raise capital more easily (by sales of stock and other securities) than with a partnership or sole proprietorship;
3. Ease of ownership transfer by transfers of stock; and
4. Capability of being managed professionally.

Disadvantages include:

1. Some legalities and expenses in creation;
2. More government regulation; and
3. Taxation twice for some shareholders.

To form a corporation, the incorporators (generally three) submit an application to the proper state official, usually the secretary of state. The application may be called a charter, or certificate of incorporation, depending upon the state. The charter contains the names and addresses of the incorporators; their citizenship status; the purpose for incorporating; its power, capital, and business address; and names and addresses of the directors. When the state accepts the charter, the corporation is "born."

Ownership in a corporation is documented by capital stock certificates. The IRS says, "Forming a corporation involves a transfer of money, property, or both by the prospective shareholders in exchange for capital stock in the corporation."[6]

Sylvia adds the following aspects unique to corporations: (1) They can provide medical reimbursement for employees; (2) they can provide qualified pension programs of up to 25 percent of the salary.

She cautions that the IRS does not allow incorporation for tax purposes. However, it can be for general business purposes, or to institute limited liability, for example. A charter operator should remember this if asked during an audit, "Why did you incorporate?"

C corporations file federal taxes on either Form 1120 or Form 1120-A (short form).

S Corporation

An S corporation is a blend that offers the same limited liability as does a C corporation. However, it passes profits and losses through to the shareholders much like a partnership does for partners, thus avoiding double taxation. (The "S" is for "small" business, although a small business can incorporate either as C or S.)

An S corporation is subject to more governmental regulation than a C corporation. An S Corporation cannot provide medical reimbursement for employees. And the only corporate retirement plan allowed is the Keogh plan. There is also a limitation on passive corporate income.

For many small businessmen, the advantages of an S corporation far outweigh the disadvantages. Linda Sylvia, stating that small business is the backbone of America, explains that S corporations employ more people than the large C corporations, and that they bring in more gross receipts.

For federal tax returns, an S corporation files Form 1120S and provides an individual copy of Schedule K-1 to each shareholder, in the same manner that a partnership does for each partner.

Naming Your Business

Plan ahead. "Jones & Son" might be about as appropriate as a wooden ship's figurehead on a fiberglass dinghy if Jones's son decides to join the navy and his daughter stays home to help run the business. Similarly, "Jones Charters" might become meaningless if Jones and spouse convert to a yacht sales business. "Jones Charters and Brokerage" might cause confusion at least, and legal heartburn at worst, if "Jane's Charters and Brokerage" happens to be an old-line operation down the wharf.

You can legally change business names relatively easily, and a change might entail nothing more than new stationery and checks, but it could also mean a new address, or even an amendment to a partnership agreement or a corporate charter (see following section).

If you decide to incorporate, your business name will be filed with the corporate papers. If you don't incorporate, and your business will use any name other than your own, you must file a fictitious-name statement.

To obtain approval for a fictitious name, you normally pay a small fee, have your proposed name checked for possible duplication, and advertise four consecutive weeks your intention to "do business as" (dba), for example, "Jones Yachting Services." Save money by advertising in a weekly neighborhood paper instead of the city paper. In many communities, small papers print fictitious-name notices for a substantial part of their advertising income and can handle the details quickly over the telephone.

Your Business Location

Do you plan to work out of a boat? A dockside office? Your home? Will you use a post office box for a mailing address? What location will attract customers, is within your business-plan budget, and falls within the zoning and licensing regulations?

If your business will operate from an office or a building, here are some questions[7] the Small Business Administration (SBA) suggests you ponder:

1. Will you have enough room when your business gets bigger?
2. Can you fix the building the way you want it without spending too much money?
3. Can people get to it easily from parking spaces, bus stops, or their homes?
4. Have you had a lawyer check the lease and zoning?
5. Have you made plans for protecting your store against thefts of all kinds—shoplifting, robbery, burglary, employee stealing?
6. Have you talked with an insurance agent about what kinds of insurance you need?

Regulations, Licenses, Zoning, and Permits

Although exact regulations for businesses vary from state to state, certain general requirements will have to be met. The chamber of commerce or the local SBA office can provide specific information. A telephone call or a visit to the city and county licensing and zoning departments can also strip away a lot of confusion.

When applying for a license, be careful about the terminology you use to describe the potential business. For example, the license needed to run a bait shop that rents out johnboats can be very different from a license for operating a fishing guide and charter service. General requirements follow.

City and County

You will need a business license from one entity, or perhaps both. Accountant Sylvia advises that a business license serves two purposes: (1) It gives the operator legal authority to conduct business; (2) if the business is making little or no profit, a license is one indicator to the IRS that the operator is truly in business—and rates business write-offs—and is not merely pursuing a hobby.

You will also want to be sure you are conducting business in a place that is zoned for your type of charter operation.

State

The state will probably require that you file for a sales and use tax number. You should also obtain appropriate publications for filing state income and unemployment taxes, and disability or medical taxes if appropriate. If the business is not a corporation, and you are doing business under a name not your own, you will have to register for a fictitious name (as mentioned earlier), either with the state or the county, depending upon state regulations.

Federal

Contact the IRS for a business tax kit. This will include forms and publications for your particular business entity. It also explains procedures for obtaining an employer's identification number (EIN) and for paying estimated income taxes, FICA (Social Security) taxes, and federal unemployment taxes. Most businesses need an EIN whether or not they hire employees. A sole proprietorship will probably need an EIN only if it hires employees.

In addition to preparing business tax kits, the IRS periodically holds small business seminars. Call the local IRS number to inquire about dates and places.

Other Licenses and Permits

Each boat equipped with a VHF radio must have a ship station license. If an EPIRB (emergency position-indicating radar beacon) is carried aboard, it must also be noted on the ship station license. Use Federal Communications Commission (FCC) Form 506 to apply. A local marine electronics dealer might have copies of Form 506. If not, call or write the nearest FCC office.

If your boat will depart U.S. waters, it is handy to have a valid passport. (It might be required, along with a visa, depending upon the country.) For passport information, try the number for county, state, or federal information in the government offices section of the telephone book. (Post offices have forms for passport renewals.) A travel agent should also know how to apply for a passport.

(For information on Coast Guard licenses and endorsements, see chapter on captain's licenses.)

Summary

1. It takes a combination of ability and basic business skills to succeed in a charter business or any business.

2. If you know the basics, an accountant, an attorney, and a lender can handle the details.

3. Evaluate your planned business to decide whether to operate as a sole proprietor, a partnership, a C corporation, or an S corporation. Reevaluate periodically.

4. Use a name for your business that has a chance to last for the lifetime of the business.

5. Regulations, licenses, zoning, permits, and so on, are necessary evils of being in business. Satisfy such requirements right from the beginning, so you can concentrate on running the business.

CHAPTER 4

Obtaining a Loan

S OONER or later almost every charter operator will want
a loan.[1] His chance of qualifying on the best terms and at
the best price is enhanced if he can speak some of the lender's language, and if
he knows what business information the lender thinks is important. Here's a
summary.

Types of Money

Lenders usually categorize money as *trade credit, short-term money, long-term money,* or *equity capital.*

Trade credit is money owed suppliers who permit a charter operator to carry
fast-moving inventory on open account. Fuel, provisions, ship's stores inventory, or fish bait might be carried on open account. A track record of good trade
credit is proven evidence of ability to repay borrowed funds.

Short-term loans are used for purchases of inventory for special reasons, such
as the upcoming season's inventory. Such loans are self-liquidating because they
generate sales dollars and are repaid in less than a year. A short-term loan might
be used for slower-moving ship's stores, or perhaps for a onetime publicity
promotion designed to bring in charterers during a special community celebration.

Long-term borrowing—for more than a year—provides money for expansion or modernization. Long-term money is paid back in periodic installments
from profits. A charter operator might buy a new boat through long-term credit.

Equity (investment) capital is money obtained by selling an interest in the
business. You don't repay equity capital. Instead, you take people into the
company who are willing to risk their money. They are interested in potential
income, rather than an immediate return on their investment. Equity capital often
comes from bringing in a partner or partners, or through stock sales. (See also
section below on venture capital.)

Collateral

The unsecured loan is the most frequently used form of bank credit for short-term purposes. No collateral is used because the bank relies upon the charter operator's credit reputation. That's where a good record of trade credit comes in handy.

However, many loans, both short term and long term, will require collateral. Such *secured loans* involve a signature of an endorser, co-maker, or guarantor; or a pledge of assets or securities, or both.

Types of Collateral

1. An *endorser* is contingently liable for the note he signs. If the borrower fails to pay, the bank expects the endorser to make the note good. An endorser might also be asked to pledge assets or securities.

2. A *co-maker* creates an obligation jointly with the borrower. The bank can collect directly from either the maker or the co-maker.

3. A *guarantor* guarantees payment of a note by signing a guaranty commitment. Banks often require guarantees from officers of corporations in order to ensure continuity of effective management. A guarantor for a yacht-charter operator might be the manufacturer of the yacht or yachts the operator is chartering out.

4. An *assigned lease* is similar to a guarantee. In a charter operation, the lender provides the money for a vessel. Then the buyer and seller negotiate a lease, which is assigned so that the lender automatically receives the lease payments.

5. A *warehouse receipt* is normally used for commodities. Such a receipt shows the bank that merchandise used as security either has been placed in a public warehouse or has been left on the borrower's premises under the control of a bonded employee. This type of collateral is generally used for merchandise that can be marketed readily.

6. A *trust receipt* is security for a note used in floor planning. For example, a charter operator who decides to sell a certain type of boat might arrange with a manufacturer and a lender to place models in his showroom or at his docks. He signs a trust receipt in which he acknowledges receipt of the vessels, agrees to keep them in trust for the lender, and promises to pay the lender as he sells them.

7. A *chattel mortgage* can be used to secure personal property, which can be defined as almost anything other than real estate. If a bank takes a chattel mortgage on a boat, it evaluates the boat's present and future market value to see if it will be worth the value of the principal, or more, during the life of the loan. The bank will require that the borrower have adequate hull and liability insurance on the vessel. The bank also will want to know how the borrower is going to protect it.

8. A *real estate mortgage*—for property used in the business or other property owned by the charter operator—can be used as collateral for a long-term loan.

9. *Accounts receivable,* normally for goods sold, are also accepted by many banks as collateral. In effect, the borrower is counting on his customers to pay his note.

10. *Savings accounts and credit union accounts* can be assigned to a lender for collateral. Depending upon the conditions of the loan, the borrower continues to earn interest in the savings account, thus reducing the net cost of his loan.

11. A *life insurance policy* can be assigned to a bank as collateral, usually for a loan up to the cash value of the policy. If the policy is on the life of an executive of a small corporation, a corporate resolution must authorize the assignment. Whether a borrower assigns a life insurance policy or borrows directly from the insuring company depends upon convenience, and upon the interest rate offered by each option.

12. *Stocks and bonds* can be used as collateral if they are marketable. If the market value drops below the bank's required margin, it may ask for additional security or payment.

Loan Agreement Limitations

If the lender sees your charter operation as a good risk, the resulting loan may have a minimum of limitations as to repayment terms, pledging of security, or periodic reporting. However, if he perceives the risk to be a poor one, he will seek more limitations, which will be written into the loan agreement as *covenants.* Here are some negative covenants, or restrictions on actions by the borrower that require prior approval from the lender:

• No further additions to total debt.
• No pledging or further pledging of assets.
• No issuance of dividends in excess of terms specified in the loan agreement.

Positive covenants also place limitations on the borrower. They spell out matters to which the borrower must agree, such as:

- Maintain a minimum of net working capital.
- Carry a specified amount of insurance.
- Repay the loan according to terms in the agreement.
- Supply the lender with periodic financial statements and reports.

Terms can be negotiated, and limitations in a loan agreement can be amended later, but the loan agreement you sign is one with which you might have to operate for a long time. Don't hesitate to question a restrictive clause, particularly if it is part of a preprinted form used for the loan agreement. It may be more important to your business to have it deleted than it is to the lender to keep it.

Qualifying for a Loan

After you have done all the research on the types of loans that might be available to a charter operator, collateral that might used to secure a loan, and limitations a lender might want to place on an eventual loan agreement, just what does it take to obtain a loan?

When it's time to borrow money for a charter operation, you should search for more than just a loan. You will want money for the least cost—and at the best terms possible. A carefully completed application, a thoroughly presented business plan (backed up with meaningful financial statements), and an obviously well-thought-out answer to each of the lender's questions will launch you toward your goal. (See Appendix I—How to Apply for a Small Business Administration Loan; see also chapter on the marketing plan for information on how to prepare the business plan.)

Two basic financial statements that inform a lender (and a charter operator) what the business is doing are the balance sheet and the profit-and-loss statement. (See chapter on accounting and budgeting.) The balance sheet is the major yardstick for solvency, and the profit-and-loss statement for profits. A series of these two statements over a period of time is the principal device for measuring financial stability and growth potential. An accountant can prepare these statements, but as a charter operator, you will need to understand them.

In addition to the normal methods of evaluating financial statements, the lender will be especially interested in the following elements:

• General information. What is the condition of accounts payable and notes payable? What are the salaries of the owner-manager, the partners, and/or the officers? Are all taxes being paid currently? What is the number of employees? What is the insurance coverage?

• Accounts receivable. Have some of the accounts receivable already been pledged to another creditor? What is the accounts receivable turnover? Is the accounts receivable total weakened because many customers are far behind in their payments? Has a large-enough reserve been set up to cover doubtful accounts? How much do the largest accounts owe and what percentage of the total accounts does this amount represent? Does the accounts receivable include anticipated seasonal or return charterers? If so, are these covered by contracts? With deposits? By customer history? With reserves in the event of adverse weather, airline strikes, or other unforeseen events?

• Fixed assets. List the type, age, and condition of the boat or boats. What are the other fixed assets? What are the depreciation policies? What are the details and conditions of existing liens? What are the future acquisition plans?

• Profit and loss. Is the profit margin adequate? Is the operator doing a lot of business yet showing a lack of profit, thus indicating that expenses are not controlled? Are profits dropping because of sagging sales? Is the market insufficient? What is the break-even point for profits?

• Estimate of future profits and losses. Is the operator's forecast of cash income and expenditures realistic?

For the bottom line, the lender has to decide three things:

1. Does the charter operator truly need money, or is he trying to put a financial Band-Aid on a management problem? Here's what the SBA says:

> Poor management is the reason why some owner-managers of small firms have trouble when they try to borrow. In spite of respectable sales volumes, many owners of small businesses run into financial trouble. Often these owner-managers have three things in common. First, they know their line of business. Their technical ability is first rate. Second, they are poor managers. In many instances, they fail to plan ahead because of their enthusiasm for the operating side of their business. In the third place, most of them feel that additional money will solve their problems. Often a bank lending officer refuses or "declines" the loan request of such manager-owners.[2]

2. Does the charter operator really know what kind of money he needs, how much, and why?

3. Can he pay back the loan?

If your request for a loan is turned down, the SBA advises that the best bet is to accept the refusal gracefully and look for weaknesses in the presentation. You can correct those weaknesses when applying for a loan in the future.

Venture Capital[3]

A charter operator seeking a large amount of equity capital—generally between $250,000 and $1,500,000—might contact a *venture-capital firm*. Venture-capital firms are interested only in large projects because of the high cost of investigation and administration.

Venture capital is a risky business for the lender, because it is difficult to judge the worth of a company in its early stage. Therefore most venture-capital firms set rigorous policies for acceptance. The typical venture-capital firm receives more than a thousand proposals a year, rejects 90 percent of them, and investigates thoroughly the remaining 10 percent. The investigations, costing from $2,000 to $3,000 per company, result in perhaps ten to fifteen proposals of interest. After further investigations, the firm might invest in one or two of these.

Whereas banks look at a business's immediate future, while being influenced most heavily by its past, venture capitalists look to its longer-run future over a five- to seven-year period. They invest for long-term capital growth, not for interest income. Thus, they are owners. They hold stock or other securities in the company, adding their invested capital to its equity base.

Although venture-capital firms may provide money through direct stock ownership, they more likely will provide it in some interim form—convertible subordinated debentures, preferred stock, or straight loans with options or warrants. They probably also will insist on having a say in major business decisions, and will likely lead the operator on the road to eventually selling out or going public.

Venture-capital firms include:

• Traditional partnerships, often established by wealthy families.
• Limited partnerships and other professionally managed pools of institutional money.
• Investment banking firms.

• Insurance companies, which often require a portion of equity from smaller companies as protection against inflation.

• Manufacturing companies.

• Small Business Investment Corporations (SBICs), which are licensed by the SBA.

• Individual investors.

More Information

For a list of information available from the SBA, see Appendix G—Government Publications for Charter Operators. See also chapter on yacht management for loans packaged with sale and lease-back arrangements.

Summary

1. Trade credit is open account credit. Short-term loans are self-liquidating through sales. Long-term loans are similar to car payments and mortgage payments.

2. Equity capital comes from selling part of the business.

3. Loans can be unsecured, or they can be secured by a variety of collateral.

4. A charter operator should seek more than just a loan; he needs to obtain the best possible terms.

5. A loan officer will judge a charter operator's borrowing qualifications by the way he applies for a loan, and by the condition of his accounts.

CHAPTER 5

Accounting and Budgeting

O N payday a professional captain deposits his check in the Seamen's Bank and withdraws part of the total. He stops by the Old Watering Hole and buys himself a drink and one for his buddy. He springs for two boiled-lobster dinners, and another round of drinks. Then he leaves the Watering Hole with enough cash left to pay his rent, buy gas for his pickup truck, and pay for enough groceries to last until the next payday. He climbs into his truck and heads for home, happy that his checking account balance remains large enough to handle short-term emergencies, and that his savings account nest egg is growing.

The captain has just performed basic accounting, much like many of us do every day. He knew how much money he had on hand and in the bank, and he budgeted his income and expenses. He also had a handle on long-term assets and possible liabilities.

A charter operator must handle accounting more formally, simply because business transactions get too complicated to remember. You don't have to operate as a PA or a CPA, because you pay your accountant for that, but to have a chance for success, you need to do two things:

1. Keep certain records; and
2. Convert the records, or have them converted, into understandable summaries.

These summaries will answer the questions, "How did I get here?"; "How am I doing?"; and "Where am I going?" They also can be used for preparing tax returns for the Internal Revenue Service (IRS).

Keeping Records

In order to start keeping records as a charter operator, you will have to make three decisions to fit your particular operation. You need to determine an *accounting period* and an *accounting method*; and you need to decide upon a systematic way to record your accounting—a method of *bookkeeping.*[1]

Accounting Periods

Records can be summarized monthly, seasonally, annually, or at any other times. However, the IRS requires that each business prepare returns on a tax-year basis. Thus, it is generally simpler to dovetail business accounting periods with the IRS tax year. A tax year can be a calendar year, a fiscal year, or a "short tax year."

A calendar year, obviously, runs from January 1 through December 31.

A fiscal year can be any consecutive twelve-month period ending on the last day of any month except December. It also might be a "52-53-week year" if you close your accounts, say, the first Monday in September. A seasonal charter business might operate on a fiscal year, or 52-53-week-year basis, with the year ending at the close of the season.

A short tax year is a tax year of less than twelve months; this occurs if the business is not in existence for an entire tax year, or if it changes its tax year.

Although the tax laws are continually being modified, here are some general guidelines:

• A business that does not maintain a set of books and records must use the calendar year.

• A sole proprietor must use the same tax year as his personal tax year, unless the IRS grants permission to do otherwise.

• In a partnership where the principal partners (those having an interest of 5 percent or more in partnership profits or capital) do not all have the same tax year, an IRS counselor or an accountant should be consulted.

• Any service corporation formed January 1, 1988, or later must use the calendar year.

• S corporations (see chapter on starting your business) must use the calendar year unless the corporation can establish a business purpose for having a different tax year.

• C corporations that are not service corporations establish their tax year when they file their first income tax return. For example, the filing of a calendar year return or a short-tax-year return ending on December 31 establishes a calendar tax year for a C corporation.

Accounting Methods

Do you account for income when you earn it or when you receive it? Do you account for expenses when they are due or when you pay them? The answers will help you determine which accounting method to use. The IRS says:

> No single method of accounting is required of all taxpayers. You must use a system that clearly shows your income and deductions and you must maintain records that will enable you to file a correct return. In addition to your permanent books of account, you must keep any other records necessary to support the entries on your books and tax returns.[2]

Accounting methods generally will be either a *cash method* or an *accrual method*, although any other method that clearly shows income—including combinations of cash and accrual—can be used.

With the cash method, you include in your gross income all items of income (including property and services) you actually or constructively receive during the year. (Income received constructively is income credited to your account or made available to you without restriction as to the time and manner of payment.)

If you use the cash method of deducting expenses, you usually are expected to deduct them in the tax year in which you pay them. However, expenses you pay in advance can be deducted only in the year in which they apply.

Under the accrual method, all items of income are included in your gross income when you earn them, even though you may receive payment in another tax year. Expenses are deducted when you incur them, whether or not you pay them in the same year.

Bookkeeping[3]

Unlike the professional skipper mentioned at the beginning of this chapter, who kept his accounts in his head, most charter operators have to do their accounting on paper. They need a bookkeeping system, which can be either single- or double-entry. A single-entry system is the simplest to maintain, while a double-entry system can ensure accuracy and control over larger charter operations because of built-in checks and balances. Below is an overview of each.

Single-entry bookkeeping accounts for the flow of income and expenses through the use of daily and monthly summaries of cash receipts, and a monthly summary of disbursements. Thus, in the simplest form, a beginning bank balance, plus income, minus checks written, should equal the new bank balance.

In double-entry bookkeeping, transactions are first entered in a journal and then are posted to ledger accounts. Each account has a left side for debits and a right side for credits. The system is self-balancing because every transaction is recorded as a debit entry in one account and as a credit entry in another. Thus, after the journal entries are posted to the ledger accounts, the total of the amounts entered as debits must equal the total of the amounts entered as credits. An imbalance in accounts indicates an error, which can then be found and corrected.

Thou Shalt Not Commingle Funds

No matter which bookkeeping method you use, accounting and tax planning expert Linda Sylvia warns that you should have a separate, business bank account for your chartering business. If you commingle funds (like shoving a charter fee into your pocket, then using it to pay your personal grocery bill), your records can become meaningless. Such sloppy accounting can lead the IRS to suspect you of hiding profits, on the one hand, or merely operating a hobby (and thus ineligible for business write-offs), on the other. A separate bank account avoids these problems, and it provides the machinery for the basic accounting arithmetic cited earlier: Beginning bank balance, plus income, minus checks written, equals new bank balance.

Petty Cash

Even with a business bank account, many expenses will have to be paid in cash. Failure to control and record these miscellaneous monies can bilge the bookkeeping system before it even gets underway. For several years while I was in school, I worked part-time as a newspaper carrier and collected payments from my customers once a month.

Under my contract with the newspaper office, I would use the first funds collected to pay for the papers (the overhead) and keep the remainder as profit. Before starting to collect, I would withdraw $10 in nickels, dimes, and quarters from my bank account, to be sure I could make change. Each evening during collections week, I would treat myself at a bakery located along the route, paying from the ditty bag full of change. My monthly profits always seemed to come up about $10 short.

I wasn't handling my petty-cash account properly, and thus was stealing from my business and reducing profits.

Accountant Sylvia outlines two ways to avoid such an outcome in a chartering business:

1. Cash a check for a minimum usable amount—say, $50. Keep the money separate from the cash in the register drawer. (A cigar box or any other suitable-size box works well.) As money is needed, withdraw it from the petty-cash fund and replace it with a receipt. Thus, at all times the petty-cash fund contains $50 in cash and receipts. If you remove money for personal purposes, mark a petty-cash receipt "DRAW," and place it in the petty-cash box. When the cash on hand runs low, total the receipts by *category* (i.e., office supplies, tolls, and so forth). Write a check payable to petty cash for the total amount of the receipts, and list the categories and amounts on the stub. The petty-cash fund now has $50 cash on hand.

2. The second approach works well for a charter operator on the run. Pay for miscellaneous purchases out of pocket, and place the receipts in a box or other container. Occasionally, or perhaps once a month, sort out the receipts by category and write yourself a check, annotating the stub with the categories and amounts. With this method, the business is never out a penny, and the accounting is as secure as a double-clamped hose.

The Watch Doesn't End until You Complete the Log

We're not talking now about deck logs or engineering logs. We're talking about logs the IRS insists a charter operator keep if he uses a vehicle or a computer part-time in his business. Failure to keep such a log can be as serious as a leaking through-hull. Accountant Sylvia explains that if an operator claimed automobile expense mileage, for instance, and couldn't produce a log, the IRS could label the entry fraudulent, as opposed to merely disallowing the claim. Sylvia says, "You had better darn sight have a log, kept at or near the time the use took place."

For a vehicle, keeping a simple form under the seat to record business use of the vehicle can be an easy solution. It might be set up in columns as follows:

	Time			*Mileage* (Odometer Reading)			
Date	Start	Finish	Total	Begin	End	Total	Remarks

For a computer, the log should show times of personal use as well as times of business use. It could be kept near the computer, or could be done in a computer file. A computer log might be set up like this:

Date	Start	Finish	Purpose	*Hours* Business	Personal

A Bottom-Line Basic Accounting System— Two Cigar Boxes

An operator of a large charter business might have his own accounting department, complete with dedicated computers and associated software, busy making daily closeouts and balances and producing massive printouts for each division. However, an operator of a smaller business might collect accounting information as transactions occur, manually sort it by category, and convert it or have it converted into understandable summaries once a month. SCORE chapter president Lester M. Unger puts it this way: "You can hire bookkeepers or do it yourself with two cigar boxes."

Accountant Sylvia has explained how it works:

• Box 1—Income. Use a receipt book for all income received. Record categories of income on the receipts, such as "charter fee," "soft drink sales," etc. Transfer all money from the box to a business checking account. Keep the receipts in the box until time for summarizing.

• Box 2—Expenses. Using the business account's three-per-page checkbook, write checks for all expenses and annotate categories of expenditures, such as "fuel," "loan payment," and so forth, on the stubs. Attach to the corresponding check stubs any bills and statements received. (Remember to use a receipt system to account for petty cash, as explained previously.) Keep check stubs in the box until time for summarizing.

• Result. Basic single-entry bookkeeping, with each transaction documented: The beginning bank balance, plus income, minus checks written, equals the new bank balance. The categorized amounts of income and expenses can be converted into understandable summaries.

Understandable Financial Summaries

Whether accounting takes place with two boxes or via a more complicated method, the results can be used to answer those three important questions: "How did I get here?"; "How am I doing?"; and "Where am I going?" The profit-and-loss statement (or income statement), along with the balance sheet (or net worth statement), can tell you (and your lender) how you got there and how you are doing. They can also show where operational changes should be made. An *operation projection* can incorporate changes and show where you are going.

Profit-and-Loss Statement (P&L)[4]

The P&L presents a summary of the financial transactions of the business during a stated period, whether it be a month, six months, or a year. It indicates (1) the income earned from chartering fees, from merchandise sales if any, and from any other source connected with the business; (2) all expenses incurred during the period; and (3) the net result in the form of profit earned or loss incurred for the period.

But the P&L goes beyond merely listing income, expenses, and the difference between them. It offers a chance to compare operations against the previous period or periods. It also provides a tool for obtaining the most efficiency from the expense dollar by analyzing and subsequently reducing expenses. And it can show how to maximize profits by combining sales volume with cost control. In short, it tells you where you are, and how you got there; and it gives you a good idea of how you are doing.

Some aspects of the financial picture of a charter operation may be as obvious as a fifteen-degree list. The hypothetical ABC Chartering Company's annual P&L, shown in figure 1, provides several examples.

Figure 1. Profit-and-Loss Statement
ABC Chartering Company

GROSS SALES		70,000
COST OF SALES		
Opening Inventory	13,000	
Purchases	<u>25,000</u>	
Total	38,000	
Ending Inventory	<u>14,000</u>	
TOTAL COST OF SALES		<u>24,000</u>
GROSS PROFIT		46,000
OPERATING EXPENSES		
Payroll (not including owner)	26,000	

Dock and office rental	3,000
Payroll Taxes	1,500
Interest	2,250
Depreciation	5,250
Telephone	2,400
Insurance	1,000
Miscellaneous	1,000
Total	42,400
NET PROFIT (before owner's salary)	3,600

Extrapolated from SBA MA 1.010: *Accounting Services for Small Service Firms*, by Irving M. Cooper, member of Cooper, Weinstein and Kumin, Certified Public Accountants, Worcester, Massachusetts.

An accountant[5] might analyze ABC's P&L as follows:

To begin with, the year's net profit $3,600 does not warrant the time and effort that the charter operator is contributing, unless he is in business just to pay for his boat. In that case, he paid $2,250 in interest, apparently for a loan, and has $3,600 available to repay principal, and to eat.

The charter operator should analyze his low profit figures by breaking down sales and expenses into two categories: merchandise and charter fees. Then he can compare expenses as percentages of sales for each category, as shown in figure 2.

Two trouble spots show up in figure 2 like quick-flashing lights. One is the loss on merchandise sales; the other is an excessive payroll.

Let's say that the $1,500 loss on merchandise sales occurred because the operator did not price his inventory properly. He received a 30 percent discount when he bought the items, but sold them at barely more than cost, perhaps believing that the ship's store would carry itself while attracting charter customers. He should have set the sales price—provided competition allowed it—at $34,286 ($24,000 divided by 70 percent equals $34,286) instead of $25,000. This markup price would have covered costs and would have given a net profit of $7,786 ($10,286 minus operating expenses of $2,500).

Now look at the other trouble spot. More than 57 percent of the charter fee income is spent for payroll, and that does not include the charter operator's salary. Therefore, the operator needs either to increase charter fees, or to make more efficient use of the employees.

Figure 2. Profit-and-Loss Statement—Expenses as Percentages of Sales

ABC Chartering Company	Total		Merchandise		Charter Fees	
	Amount	Percent	Amount	Percent	Amount	Percent
GROSS SALES	70,000	100.00	25,000	100.00	45,000	100.00
COST OF SALES						
Opening Inventory	13,000		13,000			
Purchases	25,000		25,000			
Total	38,000		38,000			
Ending Inventory	14,000		14,000			
TOTAL COST OF SALES	24,000	34.29	24,000	96.00		
GROSS PROFIT	46,000	65.71	1,000	4.00		
OPERATING EXPENSES						
Payroll (not including owner)	26,000	37.14			26,000	57.78
Dock and office rental	3,000	4.29	1,500	6.00	1,500	3.33
Payroll taxes	1,500	2.14			1,500	3.33
Interest	2,250	3.21			2,250	5.00
Depreciation	5,250	7.50			5,250	11.68
Telephone	2,400	3.43	100	.40	2,300	5.11
Insurance	1,000	1.43	400	1.60	600	1.33
Miscellaneous	1,000	1.43	500	2.00	500	1.11
Total	42,400	60.57	2,500	10.00	39,900	88.67
NET PROFIT (before owner's salary)	3,600	5.14	(1,500)	(6.00)	5,100	11.33

Extrapolated from SBA MA 1.010: *Accounting Services for Small Service Firms*, by Irving M. Cooper, member of Cooper, Weinstein and Kumin, Certified Public Acountants, Worcester, Massachusetts.

Is he passing payroll costs of his captains through to the customers? Is he paying charter wages to his captains even when they are between charters? Is he paying excessive wages out of loyalty to employees? Should he pay by the hour, the job, or the month? Does he often find himself sitting in a deserted ship's store while he's paying an employee to take a boat somewhere?

The $2,300 telephone bill charged against charter fees also needs a review. Since there is no advertising cost, maybe he uses the telephone to draw customers. If so, perhaps he can find a way to advertise through the mails, and thus reduce long distance telephone calls.

If the ship's store is to continue, the average inventory might be cut, in order to free up some operating funds. The average inventory for the twelve-month period is $13,500 ($13,000 opening inventory, $14,000 ending inventory, $13,500 average inventory). With the cost of sales being $24,000, the average inventory was used less than twice a year. To put it another way, the ending inventory of $14,000 represents a ship's store supply for approximately seven months.

Knowing this, the charter operator might find ways to reduce the average inventory. Inventory control measures and comparison of unit costs can disclose which items to stock in greater quantities than others. A survey of distributors might result in arrangements for immediate delivery of some items, thus greatly reducing the need for in-store inventory.

This example of ABC Chartering Company shows the need for using percentages for analysis. The SBA explains further:

> If you increase sales and keep the dollar amount of an expense the same, you have decreased that expense as a percentage of sales. When you decrease your cost percentage, you increase your percentage of profit.
>
> On the other hand, if your sales volume remains the same, you can increase the percentage of profit by reducing a specific item of expense. Your goal, of course, is to do both: to decrease specific expenses and increase their productive worth at the same time.[6]

Another way to use P&Ls is through *break-even analysis*. Break-even is the point at which gross profit equals expenses. In a business year, it is the time at which sales volume has become sufficient to enable the overall operation to start showing a profit. Figure 3 provides an example.

Figure 3. Break-Even Analysis

	A		B	
	Break-Even Amount	*Percent of Sales*	*Profit Amount*	*Percent of Sales*
Sales	500,000	100	600,000	100
Cost of sales	300,000	60	360,000	60
Gross profit	200,000	40	240,000	40
Operating expenses				
Fixed	150,000	30	150,000	25
Variable	50,000	10	60,000	10
Total	200,000	40	210,000	35
Operating Profit	NONE	0	30,000	5

From SBA MA 1.011: *Analyze Your Records to Reduce Costs*, by Alfred B. Abraham, CPA, managing director, Business Diagnostics, New York, New York.

In statement A of figure 3, the sales volume is at the break-even point and there is no profit. In statement B for the same charter operation, the sales volume is beyond the break-even point and a profit is shown. In the two statements, the percentage factors are the same except for fixed expenses, total expenses, and operating profit.

The example in figure 3 shows that, once sales volume reaches the break-even point, fixed expenses are covered. Beyond the break-even point, every dollar of sales should earn an equivalent additional profit percentage. Again, the SBA:

It is important to remember that once sales pass the break-even point, the fixed expenses percentage goes down as the sales volume goes up. Also the operating profit percentage increases at the same rate as the percentage rate for fixed expenses decreases—provided, of course that variable expenses are kept in line. In the illustration [figure 3], fixed expenses in Statement B decreased by 5 percent and operating profit increased by 5 percent.[7]

Balance Sheet, or Net Worth Statement

The balance sheet is a listing of all assets (money and property owned by the business) and all liabilities (debts outstanding). The mathematical difference between the two is net worth. In basic terms, if a charter operator is about to go out of business, the balance sheet will reveal whether he has enough current assets to pay off current liabilities—whether he can pay his bills. However, the balance sheet can be used for more sophisticated evaluations, as will be shown. Figure 4 contains a balance sheet for a sole proprietorship.

Figure 4. Balance Sheet for Sole Proprietorship

Assets		*Liabilities*	
Current Assets		Current Liabilities	
Cash	5,000	Accounts payable	6,000
Accounts receivable	5,000	Boat loan	1,200
Inventory	5,000	Dockage	900
		Insurance	600
Total Current Assets	15,000	Total Current Liabilities	8,700
Fixed Assets		Fixed Liabilities	
Boat	40,000	Boat loan	35,000
		Net worth	11,300
Total Fixed Assets	40,000	Total Fixed Liabilities	46,300
Total Assets	55,000	Total Liabilities	55,000

Definitions. Here are definitions for the terms used in figure 4.

Current assets. Cash and other assets that can be converted to cash in a relatively short period. In the example shown, where ninety days is used, the charter operator probably expects to turn over his ship's store merchandise within that period.

Cash. Money on hand, in the till, or on deposit in a bank.

Accounts receivable. Money owed to the business and still unpaid as of the date of the balance sheet. If the $5,000 in the example is for ship's store merchandise sold by credit card, the operator is probably shipshape and watertight. If it represents signed charter contracts that he expects to execute in the next ninety days, he could be riding in a leaky boat.

Inventory. Merchandise for sale, in this case from the operator's ship's store and fuel dock.

Fixed assets (also called long-term, or slow, assets). Assets, such as the boat in the example, that probably could not be sold quickly for cash. A slow account receivable might also be shown as a fixed asset.

Current liabilities. Debts that are due for payment in a relatively short period. In the example at figure 4, ninety days is used to balance against the ninety-day period established for current assets. The charter operator has multiplied his monthly boat loan payment, dock fee, and insurance premium by three to obtain the totals shown.

Accounts payable. This is money owed to others. Although the charter operator knows what accounts these are, a loan officer, or a prospective buyer of the business would want to know what this $6,000 represents. For example, if it is merchandise or fuel, the operator is probably more stable financially than if it is a bill for a recent haul-out.

Fixed liabilities (also called long-term, or slow, liabilities). These are debts that the owner will probably not have to repay for a long period. In the example, the balance due on the boat loan as of the date of the balance sheet is shown as a fixed liability.

Net worth. This $11,300 was obtained by subtracting all other liabilities from total assets.

Working Capital. One of the most important concepts of the balance sheet is the distinction between *working capital* and *capital.* Working capital is the difference between current assets ($15,000) and current liabilities ($8,700). After paying the bills shown, the charter operator has $6,300 for reserves, contingencies, improvements to the business, and his own pay.

The *current ratio* is current assets divided by current liabilities. A ratio of 2:1 is generally considered good, while 1.5:1 is sometimes acceptable. The current ratio in the example is 1.7. The dollar value of working capital can also indicate that the business is a good risk for a short-term unsecured loan.

Capital. The term *capital*, on the other hand, represents the owner's total equity in both current and fixed assets, which in this case is net worth, or $11,300. If he obtained his boat with a $4,000 down payment, then his net worth has increased. If he has withdrawn capital in the past, then he is prospering. However, if the estimated market value of his boat, shown as $40,000, is inflated, he might be deluding himself as to the amount of his capital.

Liquid Assets. If there is any question about whether his inventory will turn over in ninety days, the owner (and prospective lender) needs to consider liquid assets as being only cash and accounts receivable (assuming accounts receivable is viable). In his case, cash and accounts receivable total $10,000, which is more than enough to pay total current liabilities of $8,700, so the owner is still in a comfortable position. Conversely, if his liquid assets were only $5,000 and current liabilities were still $8,700, he would be headed toward shoal water.

Goodwill. Goodwill is an intangible asset whose exact value can be determined only if the business is sold. A lender will seldom accept goodwill as collateral. If goodwill shows up in the balance sheet, it should be deducted from the book value of net worth, in order to obtain a total *tangible net worth*. In the example shown, if a buyer pays the owner more than the business's net worth of $11,300, he may be investing in anticipated future profits, or paying for goodwill, or both.

Balance Sheets for Other than Sole Proprietorships

Figure 4 represents a balance sheet for a sole proprietorship. If the business were a 50-50 partnership, net worth could be shown on two separate lines as $5,650 for each partner. Other partnership ratios would be shown accordingly.

A corporate balance sheet would list *capital stock* and *surplus* as fixed liabilities. Their sum would be corporate net worth. For a C corporation, another line, *reserve for federal income tax*, would be added as a short-term liability. That line is unneeded for proprietorships, partnerships, and S corporations, because they generally pay no federal income tax. (See chapter on starting your business.)

Where Am I Going—The Operation Projection (Budget)[8]

A charter operator's operation projection can be created from the following factors:

1. Anticipated profits.

2. Expected sales, including charter contracts, as well as ancillary sales of items such as ship's store merchandise, fuel, ice, bait, and so forth.

3. Fixed expenses—the costs of staying in business, regardless of whether a boat is ever let out to charter. Examples can be insurance, rent, dock fees, property taxes, wages paid to full-time employees, boat depreciation, loan interest, office expenses, and scheduled maintenance.

4. Variable expenses—costs that vary with the business volume. For instance, an increase in crewed charters can boost employee wages, whereas an increase in bareboat charters might add unscheduled maintenance costs. A change in the volume or types of advertising will cause that line item to vary. And adding live-bait tanks will create "cost of bait sold" as a variable expense.

Although sales, minus fixed and variable expenses, equals profit, other formulas can simplify projection brainstorming. For example, subtracting variable expenses from sales provides a fifth factor, which we'll call *income*. For the projection to balance, income should equal fixed expenses plus profit. Let's consider a projection with sales of $30,000, variable expenses of $16,000, and fixed expenses of $5,000.

Sales	30,000	Fixed expenses	5,000
(−) Variable expenses	16,000	+ Profit	_____
= Income	14,000		= $14,000

The profit will be $9,000. How much would sales have to increase in order to double the profit?

Sales		Fixed expenses	$ 5,000
(−) Variable expenses	_____	+ Profit	18,000
= Income	$23,000		= $23,000

Assuming that fixed expenses remain the same, and variable expenses maintain the same ratio to sales, then sales must still be 214 percent of income. 214 percent times $23,000 equals $49,220. Hence:

Sales	$49,220	Fixed expenses	$5,000
(−) Variable expenses	26,220	+ Profit	18,000
= Income	$23,000		= $23,000

At this stage, the charter operator can evaluate how he might increase sales to $49,220. If the total number of charter days he expects to sell for the season won't support this increase, he can consider increasing charter fees. And he needs to look carefully at the variable expenses. If, for example, he can find a way to reduce variable expenses by $25 per charter day, and he anticipates 165 charter days for the season, he will increase income by $4,125, which increases profits dollar for dollar.

You can start a projection either by forecasting sales and working down, or by forecasting profits and working up. Using the system shown, once all possibilities have been considered, if income equals fixed expenses plus profit, the projection is workable.

Although an initial projection might seem to involve a lot of guesswork, a counselor from the Small Business Administration or from SCORE, or your accountant, can assist with estimated percentages from similar operations.

The year-end financial summaries will offer a chance to fine-tune that year's operations as a planning tool for the subsequent year. For a start, the summaries will show you whether the present profit is large enough to provide a return on investment and give you a salary for your work. At that point, you should be careful about concluding, "I'm satisfied, because the business made my boat payments and fed me last year." As sure as Neptune lives in the sea, if that's *all* the business does for you, you need to establish a better operation projection, or consider employment that will pay for the boat, feed you, *and* pay you a salary.

Cash Flow[9]

Most charter operators should also use a second projection (budget) called *cash flow.*

A cash-flow projection is a listing of anticipated income and expenses, with a breakout to show that enough cash will be on hand to pay each month's expenses. For instance, if you must pay dockage semiannually, your cash projection might allow for monthly accumulations of cash to cover the lump-sum payment. You might also accumulate funds for annual haul-out fees—or, conversely, make arrangements with the yard for monthly billings. In another example, if your chartering business is seasonal, the cash-flow projection can ensure that you will have funds for fixed expenses that occur during the off-season.

Other Budgets[10]

Larger businesses need more projections than the type just described. These can include projections with labels such as expenses, administrative expenses, income statement, projection of collections of accounts receivable, and half a dozen more. When it's time for more projections, your accountant should advise you.

Summary

1. Necessary accounting means keeping records that can be converted to understandable summaries.

2. The summaries should answer the questions, "How did I get here?"; "How am I doing?"; and "Where am I going?" The profit-and-loss statement, the balance sheet, and the operation projection will do this for you.

3. It is efficient to use accounting summaries in a form that allows for income tax preparation.

4. Accounting methods are generally cash and accrual.

5. Do not commingle funds. Business funds belong in business bank accounts.

6. Control and record petty cash.

7. For many charter operators, accounting can be as simple as two cigar boxes, one for income and one for outgo.

CHAPTER 6

Insurance

R ON WAHL, founder of Sea School, a national Coast Guard license prep organization, says that newly licensed charterboat operators often ask him what insurance they must have. His reply: "None is required by law. It just depends upon what you are willing to risk." Couple that answer with the fact that lenders demand insurance, and the result is that most charter operators must be insured.

Although marine insurance terms can sound radically different from terms found in homeowner's and automobile policies, the protection needed by a charter operator is straightforward. Normally you would seek:

1. Insurance for the boat and its equipment, generally called hull and machinery insurance.

2. Insurance for cargo carried for hire.

3. Liability insurance, called protection and indemnity (P&I).

Hull and Machinery Insurance

The underwriter needs to know everything about the boat— age, construction materials, condition, electronics, navigational systems, firefighting systems, engine, type of fuel, where operated, who operates it, and on and on.

He obtains this information from a marine surveyor, who is hired by the owner. The surveyor's report should list minor problems as well as major ones. Normally, if the owner shows proof that the major problems have been corrected, the underwriter will insure the boat, provided that:

• The operator or operators are satisfactory, e.g., licensed captains, with appropriate experience for the boat;

• The boat will be used for the purposes for which it is insured, and is documented and inspected accordingly, if required (see chapters on boat licenses and inspected vessels); and

• The boat will be operated in waters for which it is insured.

It should be noted that a prospective buyer can use a survey report as a negotiating instrument for the sale. When the buyer gets the report, he can ask the seller to resolve the major problems—and even the minor ones—as a condition of sale. Then, if he consummates the sale, he can use the results to obtain his insurance.

Obviously a good, objective marine surveyor is important to buyer, seller, and underwriter. Wahl urges, "Pick your surveyor like you would pick a surgeon for a heart bypass."

Granted, surveyors don't sport degrees or flaunt licenses (neither local licenses to do business nor Coast Guard captain's licenses indicate proficiency as a marine surveyor). Their only formal qualifications might be course completions in design or maintenance. And they might be members of professional organizations.

But, like heart surgeons, a substantial measure of their qualification comes from their experience, and from word-of-mouth reports by people who have used them. In short, if Dr. Heartfixer has done two hundred successful bypasses, you might select him to do yours. If Captain Nitpicker has surveyed Offshore 33 sloops for ten years, you might want him to survey an Offshore 33 for you.

But where do you find Captain Nitpicker? Some insurance companies keep a list of surveyors whose work they know and trust. Brokers, boatyard managers, lenders, and friends with boats will also have names. Also try "Surveyors, Marine" in the Yellow Pages. When you find Captain Nitpicker, question him about his background and his fees (generally by the foot), and check his references.

The surveyor should go over the boat in the water as well as out, and should inspect and try *everything*. That includes engine, through-hulls, seacocks, plumbing, electrical, electronics, ground tackle, rigging, lifelines, hull, shaft, prop, cutlass bearing, rudder, operating systems—*everything*. When he's through, he should have a combination X ray, CAT scan, and lab report of your boat.

Insurance for Cargo

Cargo insurance is available to the charter operator/owner, the shipper, the receiver, and the consignee. An operator/owner who customarily carries cargo might want an "open policy," whereas an operator who normally carries only passengers might consider single-occasion cargo insurance when necessary.

Liability Insurance—Protection and Indemnity (P&I)

P&I generally covers all liabilities resulting from the operation of the boat except physical damages to the vessel itself, damage to property owned by the insured, and losses payable under the hull policy.

What Charter Operators Can Do about Insurance

Insurance planning must be part of the earliest stages of the business plan. Insurance can be expensive, and hard to get. The consensus of other charter operators is that you should (1) do everything possible to make your operation insurable at an affordable cost, (2) shop around for prices and coverage, and (3) investigate agencies and underwriters to ascertain whether they are likely to stay in business, and thus are likely to fulfill future claims to your satisfaction.

Look for Group Rates

Dive-boat and dive-shop operators can generally count on the major certifying agencies for insurance availability (see Appendix D for partial list). The American Water Ski Association offers insurance for its members. Some charter clubs and owner associations, and some insurance underwriters, are affiliated with organizations that arrange group insurance. Check through the trade magazines for your type of charter business. And don't forget the Yellow Pages and your local reference librarian.

Insurance for the Deductible

Several charter operators report that they buy hull insurance that has a deductible and then collect the amount of the deductible from the customers as a security deposit. For instance, Pacific Quest Charters of Vancouver (Canada) exacts a security deposit of 1 percent of the insured value of the boat—the deductible.

Establishing a Venue for Litigation

Virgin Islands Power Yacht Charters (VIP) of St. Thomas includes a clause in the charter agreement that the venue for claims against VIP will be in the U.S. Virgins. This can be effective in the case of a customer who decides to sue after he returns home. His complaint will have to be strong enough for him to decide to carry out the litigation in the charter operator's location. It further aids the charter operator in that he will not have to pay for transportation and lodging to reply to suits filed in the customer's hometown.

What Charter Operators Say about Insurance

Paul W. Fenn, president of Coastline Sailing School and Yacht Charters in Noank, Connecticut, reports: "Insurance coverage is expensive and hard to get. The best you can do is to get yourself covered as much as possible without spending an arm and a leg. Our insurance runs into five figures annually and primarily covers us for personal injury."

Fenn adds, "Insurance companies love instructors who have a license."

However, C. Van Dien, owner of International Sailing School Ltd. in Punta Gorda, Florida, says that even with licensed captains, his insurance is no less than that for bareboat companies. He adds that he had to "go out and find insurers."

Finally, there is this comment from Michael P. Twombly, owner of Shiplore Charters in Beaufort, North Carolina: "Boat insurance is a killer. Rates tripled so charter rates go up."

The Deck Log Can Be Your Best Insurance

Your log can be the best insurance in the world, whether you are defending your license, your savings, or your freedom.

Ron Wahl, founder of Sea School, who often testifies as an expert witness in admiralty cases, summarized one harrowing case:

An owner of a 65-foot steel oysterboat had a lease to fish near a main channel off the mouth of the Mississippi River. For many years he hired a captain to do the fishing. Each night the captain would anchor away from the channel, using proper anchor lights.

One night a small crew boat traveling at high speed left the channel and collided with the oysterboat. The crew boat was going so fast that it ran up on the bow of the oysterboat, slamming the crew boat captain's head through the windshield. In giving testimony, the captain said he then backed his boat off far enough to observe that the oysterboat had no anchor light. Even though there was evidence of an improperly used radar on the crew boat, the captain of the oysterboat had kept no log and could find no witness from the surrounding boats to verify that he was using an anchor light on that particular night. The court found the owner of the oysterboat liable for $140,000 in medical bills.

Says Wahl, "Even if the captain hadn't logged anything that night, it still would have been important to have kept a record showing that each previous night, at a particular time, somebody customarily turned on the light. It would have shown a systematic order of things that would indicate the light might also have been operating on the night of the collision."

Wahl concludes: "If you've got a problem, don't count on getting expert help unless you've kept a logbook."

Radar Helps, but Use It

By installing certain safety devices on a boat, a charter operator often can reduce the insurance premium. A depth finder, a Loran, or an automatic fire extinguisher can qualify. However, if the insurer accepts one or more of these items, it expects the operator to keep them on board and in good working order.

Onboard radar adds another factor. If a collision occurs when the radar is not operating, the implication is that the collision might not have happened if the skipper had been using the radar. This would place the burden upon the skipper to prove he was not negligent. The moral is, if you have radar, use it any time another boat is near.

Here's the scenario of a California case that went one step further. A skipper with radar on board collided with another boat, and his insurance company paid the other captain's claim. The company then brought its own policyholder to court and recovered its loss! Why? Because the skipper could not prove he was *competent* to use the radar at the time of the collision.

John Denham, director of continuing maritime education for the California Maritime Academy, compared an incompetent radar operator with an intoxicated skipper: "In either set of circumstances, if the boat gets under way, it is in an unseaworthy condition." He explains that insurance policies are normally written to cover only seaworthy boats. In short: no competency—no coverage.

Expert witness Wahl says that a surefire way for a skipper to gain radar competency and to prove it is to get a radar endorsement on his license.

Summary

1. Insure for the amount you are unwilling to risk.

2. Group insurance can be less expensive than an individual insurance policy.

3. Regardless of premium costs, a charter operator wants to be sure his insurer will stay in business and will pay his claims.

4. The deck log can be worth a six-figure insurance policy.
5. Use radar if you have it.

CHAPTER 7

Marketing Methods

IN this chapter,[1] marketing refers to everything an operator does to promote his business, and to get customers to charter his boats and buy his products. Every charter operator is in the marketing business at all times. If a man grows a beard and wears a salty captain's cap, he's marketing. If he is clean-shaven and wears a business suit, he's marketing. A woman is marketing if she wears designer shorts and deck shoes. Ditto if she wears an executive suit. An employee who answers the company telephone is marketing. And a charter operator who spends $50,000 for advertising is marketing.

The business name is a marketing tool. So are location, personalities of captains, and the appearance and operating capabilities of the boats. In short, anything that might influence a customer or a prospect comes under the umbrella of marketing.

Many a charter operator lets a charter broker (also called agent) do the bulk of his marketing. The owner generally insures and maintains the boat and sets the charter fee; the broker finds customers for a percentage of the fees. Louise S. Dailey, president of Jubilee Yacht Charters in Darien, Connecticut, explains: "Working with a broker is to the owner's advantage, because the broker does the advertising, mails out information, checks the references, and can take care of the contracting." (See chapter on yacht management for further details.)

Listing with a broker, however, is only one marketing method. The following sections describe other methods, organized alphabetically. They are not all of the possible marketing methods by any means, because anything that works, works.

The methods discussed are advertising specialties; bulletin boards; business cards and stationery; canvassing; circulars/fliers/brochures; cross-promotions; demonstrations; direct-mail ads; exhibiting at boat shows and trade shows; magazine and newspaper ads; outdoor marketing; personal letters; point-of-purchase ads; public relations; radio ads; samples; seminars; sponsorship of events; telephone marketing; television ads; window displays; and the Yellow Pages.

62

Also included is a summary of a special technique becoming valuable in today's world of mass communication—direct marketing.

Advertising Specialties

Advertising specialties are relatively inexpensive items, such as pens, pencils, license plates and frames, bumper stickers, glassware, calendars, matches, key chains, napkins, ball caps, T-shirts, searchlights, balloons, giant tethered balloons, pennants, banners, decals, badges, and just about anything else on which you can put a company name and logo, or can use to call attention to the company.

Specialties are great for reminder advertising, particularly when an item can be keyed to the business. Some, such as giant tethered balloons, serve strictly for special promotional events, while others, which are suitable for daily use, continue to advertise. I still wear a T-shirt that announces, "I survived Lake Oologah," along with the name of the marina from which I chartered a U.S. 25 sloop in Oklahoma several years ago.

Look up "Advertising Specialties" in the Yellow Pages. Discover the old standbys as well as the latest innovations that fit your chartering business.

Bulletin Boards

You can place special signs, business cards, circulars, or even brochures on bulletin boards in targeted market areas. There should be enough copies posted so that each interested prospect can take a personal copy from the board.

Bulletin boards at marinas, bait shops, and ship's stores can be ideal spots. If located along the waterfront, or in targeted market areas, also consider restaurants, supermarkets, coin laundries, sporting-goods stores, hotels, motels, and other places where customers are likely to pass.

Business Cards and Stationery

A business card needs your name, address, phone number, logo, and motto. On the back it might carry advertising copy, or something connected with chartering that will influence a person to keep it. What about a review of Federal Communications Commission regulations for VHF radio, or a listing of the fishing bag limits, or a summary of water-skiing signals?

Every item of stationery should carry the company image—logo and motto. And stationery, like business cards, should be printed on stock befitting the image you want for your charter operation.

Canvassing

Canvassing puts you into the sales presentation business, by which you call on a prospect in order to sell a charter. A proven method of canvassing takes three steps: the contact, the presentation, and the close. During the contact you attempt to establish a relationship that will cause the prospect to welcome the presentation. The close occurs either during the presentation when the prospect indicates yes, or at the end, usually after a question that doesn't allow for a no answer.

The best contacts for canvassing come from your database (customer mailing list). Secure the leads for the database through advertising, letters, telephone calls, social clubs, and service clubs (see section on direct marketing at the end of this chapter).

Because it is a one-on-one situation, canvassing is time-consuming, but it also is inexpensive and provides direct, immediate feedback.

Circulars/Fliers/Brochures

Circulars and fliers are generally single sheets or foldovers; brochures are multipage handouts. The artwork and copy prepared for an ad can also be used for a circular (or flier), and can be a significant part of a brochure, thus spreading out the costs.

Circulars and fliers can be distributed at boat shows, from counter tops, in hotel and motel lobbies, under windshield wipers, door-to-door, at visitor welcome centers, in general correspondence, and in any other way that gets them to your targeted customers.

Save brochures for prospects who are likely to be interested. Try offering a free brochure through a small ad. Almost every return will be from an interested customer, well worth the cost of the brochure and the ad. Send the brochure, and place the customer's name, address, and phone number on your mailing list for personal-mail or direct-mail marketing.

Circulars, fliers, and brochures can be printed at less cost if ordered in quantity, and the total cost can be less than that for a large newspaper or magazine ad. Copy and artwork represent a onetime investment. Spreading the cost over a period of time makes circulars, fliers, and brochures an inexpensive method of effective marketing.

Effective? Yes. William R. Miller, owner of Miller's Suwannee Houseboats on the Suwannee River, lists a full-color brochure as the promotional program that helps his business the most.

Cross-Promotions

Frank Jordan, president of Virgin Islands Power Yacht Charters (VIP), says that by calling one phone number in St. Thomas, a customer can book one of the nine hundred luxury condominiums there, along with one of VIP's 38- to 66-foot luxury yachts. The vacationers can play golf and shop for a few days, then cruise the islands for three or four days. Jordan said that VIP's arrangement with Property Management Caribbean, a condominium management firm, has opened up a vast executive market to chartering. It was done by cross-promotion.

Cross-promotion can merge the marketing of two noncompeting organizations for the good of both. For instance, it can use one company's fliers in a second company's mailout of bills. With a specialized mailing list, it can give the charter operator better control than he gets through newspaper or electronic media advertising. And it can allow him to discount prices without losing credibility. Here's an example of maintaining price credibility:

Captain Ahab advertises his head boat for $45 per person per day but would like to obtain additional customers by discounting. If he advertises a discounted price every other week at $35, his $45 price loses credibility. Why should anybody willingly pay $45 if they know that Ahab can make a decent profit at $35? So Ahab makes an agreement with a nearby tourist-oriented hotel. He prepares fliers for the hotel, offering its guests a day of fishing for $10 off the regular price of $45—compliments of the hotel. The hotel gets a free promotional assist and Ahab gets his discount.

Demonstrations

Demonstrations should be used as tools for immediate sales. A demonstration normally runs four or five minutes, and it is followed by a closing (sales or order taking) at the end. At a boat show, a dive-boat operator might run demonstrations of a buoyancy compensation device, offered at "boat-show prices." (Boat-show discounts seldom cause a price-credibility crisis.) A water-ski operator can do the same with his equipment, as can a ship's store operator with his merchandise.

The cost of a demonstration is nothing more than the cost of using the site.

Direct Mail Ads

Direct mail is an efficient method of making charter and merchandise sales. The charter operator needs an accurate customer profile, and a database. The customer profile comes from research accomplished during step 1 of the marketing plan (see chapter on marketing plan). The database is developed from names and addresses of past customers, walk-ins, phone callers, and persons responding to your "send for free brochure" ads. An alternative to developing your own database is to buy a mailing list tailored to the customer profile, but the cost rises (see "Mailing Lists" in the Yellow Pages).

A direct-mail letter can be more persuasive if it is addressed by hand and it should be personalized with the customer's name in the salutation. It should contain a special offer, such as a discount or a gift reservation, generally with a deadline, so that you can determine the results. Use stamped return envelopes with easy-to-complete coupons. If you accept credit cards, you can expect more charter deposits, and if you have a toll-free 800 number, you can expect more returns.

A newsletter is an excellent conduit for direct-mail advertising. Imagine a "news column" explaining the great aspects of your charter business; giving dates, times, and telephone numbers; and alongside, a group of testimonials from satisfied customers—with their names and hometowns included. That's newsletter marketing.

By continually refining the customer profile and the mailing list, direct mail can become your most cost-effective marketing technique.

Exhibiting at Boat Shows and Trade Shows

Schoolchildren often have a "show-and-tell" day. If a charter operator uses a boat show for a "show-and-tell" day, he is making no money. He should use a boat-show exhibit for a "show-and-sell" day. Although institutional marketing and mailing-list development are factors, the money and time a boat show takes means that he must show and *sell*.

Distribute circulars and brochures, run a professional video showing how easy and how much fun it is to charter with Double Anchor Chartering. But sell. Offer charter reservations at "boat-show discounts" for customers who leave a deposit.

Have the credit-card imprinter and reservation receipt book ready. Be sure each person manning the booth knows how to use them. And of course arrange for a sign-up for a prize, in order to add to that mailing list.

A boat-show exhibit has to be the best you can create, or afford to have produced. A prospect judges your entire operation by the only thing he can see—your exhibit, whether it be handlettered or professionally crafted, smudgy or spotless, jury-rigged or top-of-the-line, questionable or trustworthy.

Unless you are exceptionally qualified to create your own display, find "Display Designers and Producers" in the Yellow Pages and arrange to visit a warehouse for ideas. You might be able to rent an exhibit setup, or you may want to have one constructed. Consider sharing the cost with an exhibitor whose products or services are compatible with your chartering operation.

Imagine what the competition will use; then decide whether to build your own exhibit in the garage or to purchase a professional one.

Magazine and Newspaper Ads

Written media ads can be display, classified, or classified display ads. A classified or classified display ad functions something like the Yellow Pages; people looking for *your* type of operation are likely to find it. A straight display ad, on the other hand, demands originality and proper location in order to attract attention.

To fit the marketing plan, written media advertising must tell your story, fall within the budget, and be inserted in publications read by the target customers. It should be tested, and both ads and publications should be changed when the testing so indicates.

One way to test is to advertise in several newspapers, perhaps offering a free brochure, with a different "department" in your return address for each publication, and measure results. Another method is to offer a different discount or other "special" in each publication.

A charter operator can advertise nationally and locally. (You should be aware that you can also advertise at reduced cost in the regional sections of national magazines.) However, if you own a small charter operation, you will probably do most of your advertising in regional publications pertaining to charter operations (boating/fishing/diving/water skiing), and in local newspapers in the target area.

You will want to advertise in publications where your competition routinely advertises, for two reasons. First, people are used to seeing charter advertisements in those publications. And second, the competitor must be getting sufficient return or he would not continue to advertise.

Large or small newspapers? It depends upon your customer profile and the newspapers. Test, test, test.

Here are some words that produce positive response: *free, you, results, save, sale, guarantee, proven, money, discover, health, easy, safety, now, new,* and *love.*

Outdoor Marketing

Outdoor marketing includes outdoor signs, billboards, bus and taxi signs, painted walls and roofs, banners, posters, signs on your vehicles, and names or pennants on your boats.

In the charter business, most of this marketing is indirect, and institutional. However, it can provide returns if it reaches ready customers. For instance, in a destination resort area, a charter company's sign on a bus serving a peripheral district probably would not provide a return; a sign on a tram operating a loop in the exclusive center of the resort might work.

Although billboards generally are used for instant sales ("Cold pop and beer next right."), a billboard at the edge of a fishing village announcing, "Bill's Bait Shop & Boat Rentals—Open 24 Hours—Downtown Under the Bridge" might be Bill's primary source of marketing return.

Outdoor marketing can cost little but provide a groundswell of results.

Personal Letters

A personal letter must not look like the computer-personal-ized form letters used for direct-mail ads. It should appeal to the addressee's interests by including information about him that has been gleaned from questionnaires, personal observation, the chamber of commerce, or any other source. It can end with a demand for action (*call me, stop by to talk, mail back the enclosed form with date available*), or with a statement that you will be following up in the near future.

Personal letters are relatively fast, inexpensive, and particularly suited to small businesses.

POP Ads

This is not the "pop" in a mom-and-pop charter operation. It's point-of-purchase advertising. A customer comes in to charter a houseboat on Lunker Lake and sees a sign: "The Complete Fishing Guide to Lunker Lake—On Sale Here—$3.50." On the sign are scattered pictures of bass, catfish, and crappie; it says that the book explains catch limits, how to catch, how to clean, how to cook, and everything else a charterer needs to know if he's brand-new to Lunker Lake.

Or a customer returns from a week's sailboat charter, and upon checking in with the charter operator, sees a sign: "Discounts now for charters next season."

POP ads are virtually free—many manufacturers and distributors will provide them gratis—and give instant return. Operating without them is like operating a bait shop with space for goldfish and minnows, and leaving the goldfish tank empty.

Public Relations

A successful charter operator once told me the ultimate difference between advertising and public relations: "In advertising, some guy pays someone to print, 'I'm good, trust me.' In public relations, somebody known in the community, like an announcer or a newspaper reporter, says, 'Take it from me, he's legitimate. Here's why.' "

To put it more formally, public relations is cost-effective institutional advertising that provides legitimacy because it is not paid advertising. Good public relations can increase income while reducing the advertising budget.

A charter operator has two sources for public relations: the impression he makes on customers (part of "goodwill") and newsworthiness.

Goodwill

In the chapter on liability, attorney and licensed captain Barry M. Snyder explains that most lawsuits never would have been initiated if the charter operator had used the Golden Rule of Liability: "Do unto others what you would like them to do unto you." Repeat customers and referrals are the positive result of operating with this rule.

Newsworthiness

How do you become newsworthy if you do nothing except rent boats and perform maintenance? You generate real news that is worth publicizing. For example—do something. I know a charter operator who began operating a free ferry service within the hour of the time a local bridge collapsed. His action was worth years of advertising costs—and later he was reimbursed for all costs by the community.

But newsworthy actions don't have to be that dramatic. A head-boat owner who canceled a day's fishing schedule to take passengers out to watch a special water-oriented community celebration generated news as well as fares.

Sponsor something. A fishing guide with a boat and tackle store sponsors an annual fishing contest. He gets publicity; sells bait, tackle, and boats; and sometimes wins his own contest!

A race can be automatic publicity for a powerboat or sailboat charter operator. If Twin Anchors Chartering sponsors the Twin Anchors Cup for a year or two, the publicity is there cost-free.

Join something. Match your interests and business with groups that will promote public relations: a civic club, a yacht club, an environmental group, the chamber of commerce, the Navy League, the U.S. Power Squadrons, the Coast Guard Auxiliary.

Tell the media about it. In order for that announcer or newspaper to tell the world you are legitimate, he must know about you. And he finds out through news releases (also called press releases or publicity releases), which you generate.

A news release is a typed, double-spaced factual report explaining who, what, where, when, why, and how something newsworthy happened. It should be on company letterhead, with a date of release (normally, "For immediate release") at the top, along with the name and phone number of a person to contact for further information. For print media, accompanying photography helps, if it's the type that the publication can routinely process (5×7 black-and-white print or larger, sometimes color slides, seldom color prints).

To ensure that the release goes to the right person, call the newspaper, radio, or television office and get that person's name. At a local newspaper, your release might be best suited for the sports editor, the outdoors editor, the fishing editor, or the boating editor. (On a small paper, one person might handle all of those jobs.) If your release is big news, the news editor or the city editor might want to see it. Radio and television stations have similar job descriptions—often called sports director, and so forth, all the way up to co-anchor and anchor.

There is no way in the world that you can be guaranteed that your release will be run. But it has a good chance if it indeed contains *news*. Buying a new charter boat might not be news, but buying one that is specially equipped to handle local handicapped citizens can be. Holding a weekly water-skiing contest is hardly news, but using your boats and equipment for the national finals of an American Water Skiing championship tournament is. Generate your own news.

Radio Ads

Like all advertising methods, radio ads will work only if they reach your market. Each radio station has a format—rock, country music, background music, talk, news, and the like. You will want your ads to be played by stations that use the format your customers like. And you will want them to be played when your customers are listening.

Although your research might give you a reasonable idea of customer likes and listening times, eventually you still have to test, test, test. You might advertise with three or four stations, offering a different discount on each. For example, on one station, a dive-boat operator offers free air fills for six weeks for Sunday dive-trip customers; on another station, he offers a spare-parts kit; on another, a set of dive tables. He would then measure the response to each offer, and add or cancel stations according to what the results indicate.

Listeners constantly push buttons to change stations. They are used to ignoring commercials. And they are often driving, with only half an ear attuned to the radio. To reach them, your ads should be played over and over.

Never overlook the opportunity to make radio do double duty. Wilson M. Hubbard, who owns a Gulf of Mexico party-boat and charter business, broadcasts a fifteen-minute call-in fishing-report program from 7:45 to 8:00 each morning. Hubbard reports that this is prime time for radio, particularly for this station, which reaches from the Gulf Coast to the tip of the Florida Keys.

Samples

If he has a top-notch operation, a school operator (sailing, diving, water skiing, to name a few) can offer a sample class. A charter powerboat operator might take prospects once around the bay and let them have the wheel. A fish camp operator, or a houseboat charter operator, might pass out samples of smoked fish from his river or lake.

And it works. Jack E. Ferguson, president of Marathon Divers in Marathon, Florida, reports that the promotional program that helps his business most is free boat trips and 99-cent air fills.

Minimal cost sampling can develop intense customer interest, coupled with a feeling of loyalty to the operator who provided the sample.

Seminars

A seminar is much longer than a demonstration. Think in terms of a forty-five-minute lecture, geared for a closing at the end. I attended a seminar prepared by a charter operator who offered reduced charter rates for members of his cruising club. The seminar was given by a captain who exuded cruising camaraderie like a politician exudes confidence. After explaining the advantages of club membership, he played a video of a recent cruise, showing happy sailors who happened to be wearing club patches. At the conclusion of the seminar, he obtained four family memberships from the eight couples attending, and two of the new members signed up for the next cruise. Money from both directions. Marvelous!

The seminar was given on the dock, but it could have taken place at a motel or hotel. The operator might have advertised, but he didn't need to, because the sports editor of the local paper and a local radio announcer were eager to run his news release offering a free seminar on how to cruise. In addition, he had written a few personal letters and had made some telephone calls. The seminar was exceptional because the attendees were a select market of people who *knew* they would like to cruise even before they arrived at the seminar.

Sponsoring Events

The ideal event to sponsor is one related to the chartering operation. However, some smaller communities expect their businesses to sponsor community projects. Maybe it's a Little League team, or an annual charity benefit. Comply if possible.

Telephone Marketing

A personal phone call made by the charter operator, or an assistant with a pleasing voice, is the telephone version of a canvassing campaign. Thus, it requires a contact, a presentation, and a closing. It should follow an outline but not be memorized. Rehearsal with a tape recorder will help make personal phone calls sound conversational.

A phone call takes less time than a canvass, is more personal than a letter, and is inexpensive (if local). A prospect cannot turn it down as easily as he can a letter, but can refuse easier than during a canvass.

Television Ads

A television ad has to catch the viewer in the first few seconds or it has lost him. The ad must be *visual*, supported by audio. A sailing-school ad, for instance, might present a boat under full sail in a warm, fresh wind, then cut to confident, healthy-looking people on board handling sheets. The announcer's audio meanwhile would be implying, "See how easy it is. This could be *you*." The ad would close with visual and audio repeating the company name and phone number, or address.

The cost of television advertising depends upon the time it is aired (which equates to the number of people watching). None but the biggest charter operators would consider prime time—from eight to eleven P.M., because of the expense. Some might consider fringe time, which is before and after prime time.

Costs for time after midnight become tiny, but so does the audience. And a charter operator whose customer profile is male might steer clear of daytime television, because of the preponderance of women viewers.

But there are ways to advertise to a television audience at less than prime-time cost. Time on a local TV station (either broadcast or cable) might cost less than on a major affiliate, even though it reaches the same local market. Weekend time might vary. Ads played after midnight can reach people with videocassette recorders who tape special programs and view them later.

Or perhaps you can make a deal like party-boat owner Wilson M. Hubbard did. Hubbard discusses saltwater fishing for three and a half minutes on an early breakfast TV program—early enough that bait-shop operators, fishermen, other charter operators, and even his own captains can watch before setting out for the day. Thus he enjoys prime time for his operation at much less than prime-time cost. Hubbard, who describes himself as a "waterfront character," is well enough known in the viewing area that his appearance on television is tantamount to an advertisement for his business.

Window Displays

A storefront window containing little more than your company name is like a bag of money buried in the front yard. It's not going to earn a penny.

Any charter operator can profit from window displays. Yacht charter services can display color photographs of their boats, along with special rate offerings; fishing-boat operators can display boats, motors, fishing tackle, photographs of prizewinners, and mounted trophies; dive shops and water-ski shops can present special offerings of merchandise and services.

A storefront window is a picture window looking for a display. Give it one.

Yellow Pages

People looking in the Yellow Pages are as motivated as people who attend a seminar. They are ready to be influenced to buy. However, unlike the seminar, the product or service they buy depends upon which listing or ad grabs their attention.

Must you have an ad as well as a listing? Probably, if your competition has one. And your ad can be as big as his, even though he might have four times the number of boats you operate. An equal-sized ad makes the customer see both of you as equals. If your ad is more striking, or offers more, you have the edge.

The ad ought to announce why customers should call you instead of the competition. Do you accept credit cards? Do you have a toll-free 800 number for long-distance customers? Do you offer a unique guarantee or service, unmatched by other charter operators? Hit 'em with it.

Besides deciding upon ads, consider whether to list in more than one category (fishing/bait shops, dive charters/diving certification). And as you apply the Yellow Pages to your marketing plan, you must determine how many directories to use (local, adjoining communities, customer target areas in other states).

And keep this in mind about the Yellow Pages: Any time you tell somebody you are in the Yellow Pages, you are also steering them to the ads of your direct competition. Tell them, "You'll find us in the white pages."

Direct Marketing

In this day of mass communications, where the consumer is bombarded by countless advertisements daily, marketing can be like firing a shotgun into ten thickets in hopes of scaring a rabbit out of one. Direct marketing finds the rabbit first, makes friends with it, and offers it its food of choice—a carrot.

Direct marketing establishes direct communication with prospects interested in your chartering business, thus isolating them from the mass population. It is done by direct-response advertising, asking for inquiries by phone or mail, providing coupons for redemption, and even asking for sales. It can generate information for the customer profile, while allowing for direct measurement of ad results; and it builds the marketing database.

Although direct marketing can be completed in one step—where the prospect responds by chartering—it can also be used as a two-step operation. The first step builds the database, and the second uses it.

Once the database is built, direct advertising goes to the prospects in the base. Although most methods of advertising can be used, the most adaptable are canvassing, telephone marketing, and direct mail (all explained previously).

Direct mail is the most cost-effective of the three, because letters go to many prospects simultaneously, as opposed to the "one-on-one" required for canvassing and telephoning.

Because the database forms the crux of direct marketing, this chapter and the chapter on the marketing plan refer to it often. A large, accurately profiled database is a captive market that wants to hear about your chartering operation.

Summary

1. Marketing is everything a charter operator does that influences customers to buy or not to buy.

2. Anything that works, works.

CHAPTER 8

The Marketing Plan—Core of the Business Plan[1]

FREDERICK J. ("Fritz") Regner, Jr., president of Strategic Marketing, a marketing consultant firm with offices in Ohio and Florida, advises, "You cannot afford a shotgun approach to marketing." The cost of marketing is an investment just like the cost of a boat, because a charter operator anticipates cash returns from both. As with all investment decisions, marketing choices should be based upon a careful study that uses all available relevant information. Such a study is called an integrated marketing plan. (With slight modifications and additions, the marketing plan converts to a business plan, as will be explained at the end of this chapter.)

A large charter company might need or want to hire a consultant or marketing agency to develop its marketing plan. On the other hand, in this case a small charter operator is blessed by his smallness. Not only can he develop his own marketing plan, but he also can do it accurately, because he is close to his customers, and can learn easily about their likes and dislikes. Furthermore, he can react quickly to needed change. *And* he can do this at little cost other than time.

The Marketing Plan

A logical marketing plan can be developed through these five steps, which will be explained in detail:

1. Determine your market.
2. Determine how to attract your customers.
3. Establish your marketing budget.
4. Allocate the budget.
5. Test, and modify as necessary.

Determine Your Market

To determine your market, you first need to find out who you are and who your customers are.

Who Am I? Answer questions such as these: What business am I in? Chartering? Bareboat chartering? Yacht management? Brokerage? Running a resort, a dive shop, or a fish camp, with boat rentals as a sideline? Am I doing all of the above? More? Less?

What quality of service and merchandise do I sell? Am I chartering yachts, runabouts, prams, johnboats, inner tubes? Does my ship's store sell designer boat apparel, expensive foul-weather gear, lightweight plastic ponchos, gourmet foods, light snacks?

Who Are My Customers and Potential Customers? One powerboat charter operator has determined that most of his customers are males, of any religion, thirty to forty-five years old, married with two children, in the $45,000 to $60,000 income group, unaffected by swings in the economy, have some college, take their families on vacation two weeks each summer, and are unwilling to use more than one day of that two weeks on travel time. That's his customer profile—his marketing target.

A customer profile helps you restrict your advertising to media that will reach people within that profile. To develop a profile, you need answers to such questions as: What kind of people are my customers? Where do they live? What are their zip codes and telephone numbers? What are their lifestyles? What are their sexes, ages, incomes, educations, religions, marital statuses, and occupations? What organizations do they join? What are their special interests? What do they do with their leisure time when not chartering? Why do they want to charter? How often do they charter? What do they like and dislike most about my services and products? Who do they see as my competition? What media do they use? And, most important, how many of them are there?

How does a charter operator collect this information? There are three methods, starting with internal data, and working outward. Internal data comes from records and employees. The SBA says:

> Think cheap and stay as close to home as possible . . . Look at your own
> records and files. Look at sales records, complaints, receipts, or any
> other records that can show you where your customers live or work or
> how and what they buy . . . Employees may be the best source of infor-
> mation about customer likes and dislikes. They hear customers' minor
> gripes . . . They are also aware of the items customers request that you

may not stock. Employees can probably also give you a pretty good seat-of-the-pants customer profile from their day-to-day contacts.[2]

That advice about records and employees fits charter operators perfectly. Routine business forms can easily include blanks for filling in customer information. For example, if you use a skipper's qualification checklist, you have a perfect vehicle for some of the personal information vital to your marketing plan.

Now convert the word *employees* in the SBA quote to *captains*. Anyone who has spent a day or a night on the water with someone knows that you discover things about the other person that you would never learn under any other circumstances. When a skipper brings back a charter party, at the least he can probably judge if and when they will charter again, how much they can afford, who they consider to be the competition, and how they rate the competition.

An inexpensive method of collecting data internally consists of a pad of forms and a pencil. Ask your customers and drop-ins to fill out a form, "so we can put you on our mailing list," or "so you will be eligible for our next prize drawing." Maybe the prize will be a bumper plate or a sticker, and your form will ask what kind of car they have.

If you exhaust your internal data, try secondary research. Secondary research is nothing more than the use of published surveys, market studies, census reports, research reports, books, and magazines to get the data you need.

Secondary research is not as complicated as it might seem. Most local libraries have a uniquely qualified expert who is like a computer program with a personality—a reference librarian. Tell the reference librarian what you're seeking and why you need it, and watch his or her computer drives start grinding—for free.

Other sources of secondary research material include universities and colleges, trade and general business publications, trade associations, government agencies, and newspapers.

If secondary research doesn't fill the bill, then it's time for primary research. This can include direct-mail questionnaires, telephone or on-the-street surveys, panel studies, test marketing, behavior observation, and direct marketing.

If you are using questionnaires to construct a customer profile, find ways to encourage their return. Do not ask for names and addresses. Consider self-addressed stamped envelopes, offers of small free gifts, or discounts.

Of course, without names and addresses of the respondents, you will lose a valuable source for the database (the mailing list of interested customers). A good way to collect those names is through direct marketing. Direct marketing is advertising that invites a response from a prospect by asking for phone or mail inquiries, providing coupons for redemption, and other techniques that will bring about two-way communication. It can generate information for the customer profile and the database, while allowing for direct measurement of ad results. (See chapter on marketing methods for more information about direct marketing.)

Determine How to Attract Your Customers

In order to determine how to attract customers, you must put together four building blocks. First, you have to learn about your competition. Second, you determine your position in relation to the competition. Third, you decide what image will best portray your position. Fourth, you select the marketing you must do to get that image to the customers. You can make these four decisions by answering the questions that follow.

Who Is My Competition? How many other charter operators are in my area of operations? Is the area saturated with charter businesses? How many of these firms look prosperous? What advantages do they have over me? How many look as though they are barely getting by? How many similar operators went out of business last year? Why? How many new ones opened up last year? What are the rates charged by the competing firms?

If Bootleg Charters is the major competition, find out what they do that draws customers, and what they do that loses customers. Discover which of their activities generate good profit margins and which are draining away dollars. What is their image, their strength, their weakness? Learn all you can from their experiences.

How? Sometimes Captain Bootleg himself will tell you. Or he might tell a friend of yours. Bootleg's former customers can be a gold mine of information. And so can his advertising.

What Is My Position in the Market? Knowing the competition enables you to create a *position* in the market. Your position is your uniqueness—the niche that no competitor has found, as yet. It should offer a benefit that your customers want and that is not offered by the competition. Ideally, it should be difficult to copy.

Positioning can be the most important feature of the entire marketing plan, and it can make the difference between success or failure. Consider the following examples of positioning:

Three excursion boats are operating within the same community. One boasts a rock band, stresses informality, and serves cocktails and "heavy" hors d'oeuvres. The second offers a sedate version of big-band music, requires a coat and tie, and provides dinner/dance cruises. The third dispenses with music in favor of a running loudspeaker commentary of sights being seen, and sells beer, soft drinks, popcorn, and hot dogs.

Three charter operations take place in the same marina. One operator runs a sailing school, using daysailers. The second operator charters out two 32-foot sloops as bareboats. The third rents out a fleet of small powerboats for recreational use, for guided sightseeing tours, and for fishing trips. Each operator has a long-term lease on his slips—and there are no spare slips. That's positioning.

What Image Must I Project? What kind of image do you need in order to fill your position in the market, to draw new customers, and to pull customers away from the competition? Conservative? Innovative? Exclusive? Downhome? Immaculate? Seafaring? How will you compare with the competition? Professionalism? Dependability? Willingness to serve? Prices? Strengths? Weaknesses? Unique services? Special guarantees?

What Do I Want Marketing to Do for Me? After you consider the competition, your position in the market, and the image you desire to create, you are ready to write down the message you intend to get to the customers. This message should stress the following:

1. The strong points about your particular operation.
2. Exactly how your operation differs from the competition.
3. Specific facts about your business that you will use to support (1) and (2).

Each marketing and advertising method you select after you develop your marketing budget will contain this message (see chapter on marketing methods).

Determine Your Marketing Budget

By preparing a marketing budget,[3] you estimate how much money to spend in order for profits to be worth your time and labor. There are three basic ways to do this: (1) percentage of sales; (2) unit of sales; and (3) objective and task.

Percentage of Sales. This method relates advertising directly to sales volume—which is what advertising should affect. By using percentage of *sales*, rather than percentage of *profits*, the budget is unaffected by periods of low profits that stem from factors other than sales or advertising (such as increased payroll costs or maintenance costs). The sales figures you use can be past sales, estimated future sales, or a combination.

The percentage used can be the average for the particular charter operation, adjusted up or down after measuring results.

Unit of Sales. This method is based on knowledge of how many dollars of advertising it has cost in the past to market one unit. For instance, an operator who charters out aluminum fishing boats on a lake may know from experience that it costs him $300 of advertising per season to rent one boat. Theoretically, if he owns ten boats, $3,000 in advertising will sell all ten charters for the season. Assuming that additional advertising will provide no further sales, to increase profit he must increase charter fees or lower overhead without stealing advertising dollars.

The unit-of-sales method is suitable when the amount of product available is limited, and when there are single types of merchandise whose advertising costs per sale can be measured. It would not be very useful in a ship's store that sells a large variety of small merchandise.

Objective and Task. This is the most difficult but most accurate method of establishing a marketing budget. The operator sets specific objectives, then estimates how much it will cost to reach each objective. Here's an example:

A houseboat charter operator decides to sell 25 percent more charter days on his fleet next year by attracting corporate groups. He determines what media best reach the target market and estimates the cost for running the number and types of ads he thinks it will take to achieve the sales increase. He repeats the process for each of his objectives. When he totals these costs, he has his projected budget.

If he finds that he can't afford to advertise that much, he can scale back the increase by ranking his objectives and deferring those he cannot afford.

Allocate the Budget

Once the budget has been determined, you need to decide how much of it will go to institutional marketing. Institutional marketing familiarizes customers with your trademark or logo, your slogan or motto, and your business name.

With familiarity come trust and confidence. In the customer's mind, your company becomes an old friend—and he turns to old friends when he's ready to buy. Thus institutional marketing adds competitive muscle and builds long-term sales.

Institutional marketing includes reminder advertising, but it is also an adjunct of almost every marketing method. When a prospect sees a tethered balloon with crossed anchors printed on it and says, "That's Double Anchor Charters; every boat they charter carries two complete sets of ground tackle," he is implying that he thinks your company takes better care of charter parties than others—and your institutional marketing is working.

With the institutional marketing apportioned, you can allocate the remainder for promotional advertising. Promotional marketing is directly related to sales. In its simplest form, a telephone call to a prospect that brings in a charter sale is a successful case of promotional marketing. While institutional marketing is vital for the long term, promotional marketing is the daily lifeblood of a new business—and many mature ones.

The allocation for promotional advertising can be decided by using any or all of the following five methods:

Total Advertising Budget. This might be all that a small charter business needs. However, you will probably have better control over your marketing if you include concepts from one or more of the remaining methods.

Departmental Advertising Budgets. Each department (charter, ship's store, fuel) receives dollars, generally based upon percentage of sales. This method provides the departments having the greatest sales volume with the biggest share of the budget.

Calendar Periods. You can also apply percent of sales here. If August accounts for 15 percent of sales, advertising for August might rate 15 percent of the budget. As an alternative, experience might show that August brings in 15 percent of sales regardless of advertising. This would allow for transferring some of those advertising dollars to leaner months.

Media. Past experience can help determine the best apportionment of advertising money for each of the media.

Sales Areas. Decide how much advertising should go to proven customer-producing areas, and how much to use for stimulating new sales areas.

Test, and Modify as Necessary

Investing money in marketing without testing the results is like buying a boat without a sea trial. You must find out which parts of your marketing plan work and which should be altered. You conduct your own sea trial by testing. The test takes time—perhaps six months, perhaps longer.

You can ask your customers where they heard of your company and its offerings (newspaper ad, Yellow Pages, brochure, word-of-mouth). You can use direct-marketing methods by offering discounts or small gifts for responses to coded ads. You can use marketing techniques that give instant test results (the customer either buys or doesn't buy). For every marketing method you select, he should include a plan for testing.

One charter operator offers free brochures through advertisements in a half-dozen magazines. Let's say he finds a new magazine called *Charter Vacation-lands.* He will advertise for six months, asking readers to reply to his company—attention Dept. CV-1 (to identify it as his *Charter Vacationlands* ad)— for a free brochure. If he changes the ad after six months, he changes the code to Dept. CV-2. He refines his magazines and his ads as needed, and keeps a record of responses *by name and address* to show what ads work in what magazines.

When he gets a new charter customer, he checks the name against his database to see which ad, if any, has worked. If the name is not in the database, he asks the customer where he heard about his business. Maybe one of his other marketing methods worked, or perhaps the customer is a referral.

His testing sometimes gives startling results, to which he reacts for better profits. After a long test in a major boating magazine failed to show enough return to pay for the ads, he stopped the insertions. He transferred the money to a test ad in an outdoor magazine not directly related to his charter operation, and found a prime source of customers.

Where Do I Go from Here?

So how does a brand-new charter operator who has never even bought a classified ad develop and initiate a marketing plan? He takes three steps: (1) reads; (2) carries his marketing ideas as far as possible; and (3) hires help for what he can't do.

Read

Review this chapter and the one on marketing methods. Read the appropriate Small Business Administration publications (see Appendix G). Read such books as *Guerrilla Marketing* and *Streetfighting* (see note 1). Read ads, fliers, and brochures to see how other entrepreneurs are doing *their* marketing. In particular, read the competitors' copy, and find their good points and weaknesses. Read everything from an entrepreneur's point of view.

Do What You Can Yourself

Anyone who can do ad copy, artwork, photography, layout, typesetting, or printing can save a bundle. However, be sure that the result is professional—and that it is worth your time away from running the business. Similarly, if brainstorming with ideas, or working with the print and electronic media, comes as easy as making a routine log entry, go for it.

But unless you own your own print shop and studio, and have employees to run it, you eventually will need to seek help outside the business.

Get the Right Help

Hiring the right help could be as simple as walking into one of the small desktop publishing businesses that do everything: market research, copywriting, illustration, design, typesetting. Look up "Artists, Commercial" or "Advertising Agencies" in the Yellow Pages.

While looking in the Yellow Pages, check "Marketing Consultants." Find one who welcomes a chance to develop goodwill by an inexpensive or a no-fee interview.

Visit a small local newspaper, magazine, or book publisher for ideas, and for names of people who do his illustration and layout work. Or have a talk with a printer who knows freelance writers, illustrators, and layout people looking for small jobs.

Newspaper staffs include artists and writers to assist with ads, although some marketing experts believe that such employees might not bring the individuality to your work that you want.

Radio and television staffs also can assist in their media specialties, but the same caveat about individuality applies. Try "Commercials, Radio & Television" in the Yellow Pages.

The Business Plan

1. The overall concept. Using information gained from the first two steps of your marketing plan (determine your market; determine how to attract your customers), explain the makeup of your business. Present your concept in such precise detail that someone unfamiliar with chartering could actually steal your ideas after reading it.

2. The budget. Expand the marketing budget by adding all other expenses, and calculate expenses and revenues to the break-even point. The following steps can be used to determine the break-even point and obtain a budgeted sales price, or charter fee (see chapter on accounting and budgeting):

Estimate the number of charter-days you expect per month (or per season).

Divide expenses by charter-days. If weather, maintenance, or other variables can interfere, use 75 percent or 80 percent of estimated charter-days. The result is the break-even price per day.

Add desired (or estimated possible) net profit to expenses, and divide by charter-days, to obtain the actual charter price per day.

3. Allocation of functions and tasks. If you are a sole proprietor, this is merely a matter of balancing business requirements against your skills and your number of available hours, and allocating otherwise unfulfilled requirements to employees and outside resources (such as for maintenance, crews, or accounting). In cases of multiple ownership, you should list a role for each person who is either a part-owner or a major personal investor in the business.

4. Follow the plan and modify when conditions require. A good business plan is a street sign to success when followed, a false prophet when ignored, and a forecast of failure if not changed when necessary.

Summary

1. To develop a marketing plan, determine your market and your position in it; your marketing budget; and the effect of the implementation of the budget on sales.

2. The marketing budget should consider allocations for institutional and promotional marketing.

3. The marketing plan must be flexible.

4. Use the marketing plan as the basis for the business plan.

CHAPTER 9

Liability[1]

IF you drew a line called "Owner's Liability," with a negative sign at one end and a positive sign at the other, you might regard the minus end the way the armed forces look at a commanding officer's responsibility. He is responsible for everything his unit does or fails to do. Period. No excuses.

For the positive end of the line, Barry M. Snyder, a personal-injury trial lawyer who holds a 100-ton master's license, advises charter-boat owners and captains to obey "The Golden Rule of Liability," by doing unto others what you would like them to do unto you.

Snyder explains that innumerable suits never would have been initiated if the charter operator had used the Golden Rule. A charter operator not only must care for his customers, but also must let them know he cares. He should be quick to say, "I don't think it was our fault, but let me accommodate you." The Golden Rule parallels the courts' insistence that a charter operator exercise "a very high degree of care"—a term to be reviewed shortly.

This chapter will not attempt to show you how to stay out of court. It *will* give insight into who can do what to whom in the charter business. However, any smart charter operator will get an attorney before he sets his first course in the chartering business.

Legal Actions Peculiar to the Chartering Business

Be wary of "sea lawyers" who provide free advice at docks, in marinas, in waterfront bars, and maybe even aboard your own boat. They tend to perpetuate what attorney Snyder calls a "mythology" about maritime law, making it seem bizarre and crazy. "It's just not so," he says. "Maritime law, like all other law, is based on common sense."

Maritime law differs from other law only in the types of actions that can be brought against a charter operator, a captain, or a nonliving thing called a vessel. In the actions that follow, a finding in one often can be used in another;

however, a judgment would be paid only once. Although an action may indicate that the owner, or maybe the employer, is responsible, other actions stemming from the same event can be taken against the captain, or against the vessel itself.

Seaworthiness—Owner Responsibility to Crew Members

The law holds that it is an owner's absolute and nondelegable duty to provide a vessel that is fit for its intended purposes, or the intended voyage. This makes the vessel and the owner liable in case of injury or death of a crew member due to unseaworthiness.[2] The owner is liable even if unseaworthiness occurs after the vessel leaves port, and whether or not he has notice or opportunity to correct the unseaworthy condition. However, the law does not hold the owner responsible for the negligence of the injured person's fellow crew members.

The court can find full damages against the owner, less contributory negligence (partly the fault of the crew member), excepting damages already paid for medical care, and maintenance and cure (to be discussed).

The Jones Act—Employer Responsibility to Crew Members

The Jones Act[3] takes up little more than a page in Title 46 of the U.S. Code, but its small size can be misleading. It was kept short by incorporating by reference the Federal Employer's Liability Acts (FELA), 45 U.S.C. 51-60, which apply to railroad workers. This marriage of convenience between maritime and rail workers has produced ramifications that span the seven seas.

Under the act, any seaman who, in the course of his employment, suffers personal injury due to employer negligence may seek damages from his employer through a jury trial. (An estate can also sue, in case of death.)[4] Courts have held that the term *seaman* refers to master, licensed and unlicensed hands, as well as bartenders, musicians, maids, and stewards. Damages have been awarded for pain and suffering, loss of earnings, inability to lead a normal life, and medical expenses. (However, see the section on maintenance and cure, below.)

But the cards aren't stacked entirely against the employer. Generally the court must be convinced that the employer knew, or in the exercise of due care should have known, of the dangerous condition that caused the injury or death.

Furthermore, attorney Snyder says:

Under the Jones Act, the owner can assert the defense of comparative
negligence. This means that, if the finder of fact (judge or jury) determines
that the seaman was negligent, his negligence will be subtracted from his
recovery. An example of this would mean that, if the finder of fact felt that
the seaman's total amount of damages is $100,000, but he was found to be
40 percent negligent, then his actual recovery would be $60,000.

However, Snyder warns, "If you are in a charter operation and you hire captains
who in turn hire the crews, be advised that the vessel and yourself may still be
responsible for the crew's actions aboard the vessel."

Conversely, if an operator puts a boat into bareboat charter, a party that
charters it and hires a captain or crew can also become liable under the Jones
Act. (See chapter on bareboat chartering for an explanation of how a charter
party becomes an owner.)

And, of course, any time the owner has his own employees serving aboard
his boat, he incurs liability under the Jones Act.

Maintenance and Cure—Employer, Vessel, Master Responsibility to Crew Members

Maintenance and cure $(M\&C)^5$ is like worker's compensa-
tion, in that negligence or unseaworthiness is not a factor. With certain exceptions for vessels under eighteen net tons, a seaman can seek M&C if he is injured
or taken ill in the course of employment. He can assert the claim against the
employer, the vessel, and the master. A seaman lien for damages will take
priority over a mortgage lien of the vessel.

M&C can be claimed for:

• Unearned wages;
• Subsistence; and
• Medical care.

A seaman who brings an M&C action with an action under the Jones Act will
be entitled to a jury trial.

If the crew member is on shore leave (thus on call) when the injury or illness
occurs, he will probably rate M&C, because he is still considered to be in the
vessel's service. (Vacations, however, don't count.)

Willful misconduct may cut him out of the picture. For example, judges look askance at venereal disease and at injuries resulting from intoxication. However, they often find in favor of a seaman whose injuries occur *while drinking* alcohol.

Morality is no factor. The classic case was a seaman who had had three glasses of wine and had accompanied a female to an upper room in a brothel. After a dispute over payment, he was injured when he jumped from the window rather than face his companion's male friend, who was guarding the doorway with a knife. The court awarded M&C to the seaman.[6]

Owner Responsibility to Noncrew Members

The law consistently holds that the owner has the duty of exercising reasonable care to anybody who is lawfully on board for purposes not inimical to the owner's legitimate interests and who are not members of the crew.[7] The findings include guests and others who are not crew members. The key phrase here is *reasonable care*.

The wording of the law is stricter when the owner has paying passengers on board. In the case of *Moore v. American Scantic Line, Inc.*, the court affirmed that "A steamship company is not an 'insurer' of passenger's safety but owes the duty to exercise a very high degree of care for safety of passengers."[8] This "very high degree of care" forms the basis of the "Golden Rule of Liability" described at the beginning of this chapter.

Death on the High Seas Act (DOHSA)— Vessel or Persons Responsible

The Death on the High Seas Act[9] authorizes the wife, husband, parent, child, or dependent relative of a person who died from a wrongful act, neglect, or default on the high seas to sue for damages. The suit can be against the vessel, person, or corporation that would have been liable if death had not occurred.

Contraband—Vessel and Owner Responsibility[10]

According to the law, contraband is:

• Any narcotic drug that is possessed illegally, or that has been acquired, or is to be transferred illegally;

• Any narcotic drug that does not bear appropriate tax-paid internal revenue stamps; or

• Any firearm involved with a violation of the National Firearms Act.

Contraband can end a charter operation in a heartbeat, because federal authorities—and many states—can seize any vessel involved with contraband. The law applies if contraband is aboard the boat or on the person of anybody aboard the boat. It also applies if the boat is used in any way to "facilitate the transportation, carriage, conveyance, concealment, receipt, possession, purchase, sale, barter, exchange or giving away" of any contraband article.

If contraband is proved in court, the seized vessel can be forfeited and sold, unless the owner can prove he had no knowledge of the contraband. If a charter party has the boat, the owner might still have to prove he knew nothing about it. If the charter is a bareboat charter and the charter party is involved, the owner could lose the boat even if not personally involved. (See chapter on bareboat chartering.)

Enforcement of the contraband restriction is presently very strict. The Coast Guard's policy during 1988-89 of "zero tolerance" resulted in vessel seizures for bits of marijuana residue found in passengers' staterooms. Although the policy was relaxed somewhat in 1989 for the owners of commercial fishing vessels, the message is clear: Charter operators who want to stay in business had better heed the contraband law and be sure that their customers do likewise.

Pollution—Owner and Operator Responsibility

Although this section summarizes certain federal pollution regulations, charter operators should make themselves aware of regulations promulgated by state, regional, and city authorities.

The federal Water Pollution Control Act regulates vessels and terminals and establishes liability for oil discharges.[11] The act prohibits discharge of oil or hazardous substances in harmful quantities. (Hazardous substances include plastics, and more than two dozen chemicals, including oil, gasoline, pesticides, ammonia, chlorine, and derivations.)

A harmful quantity of oil is defined as one that "violates applicable water quality standards," or, more meaningful to a sailor, causes "a film or sheen upon or discoloration of the surface of the water or adjoining shorelines, or causes a sludge or emulsion to be deposited beneath the surface of the water or upon adjoining shorelines."[12] A violation of the discharge provision of the act can rate a penalty of not more than $5,000 for each offense. In short, don't spill.

Any vessel or shore facility that discharges a harmful quantity of oil must report it to the Coast Guard. Using a carrot-and-stick approach, the act says that failure to report can bring criminal penalties, whereas reporting brings immunity from use of the notification in a criminal prosecution.[13] That doesn't prevent the government from prosecuting with other evidence.

The Water Pollution Control Act makes an owner or operator of a vessel or facility that makes a prohibited discharge liable to the United States for the costs of removal. Thus, in the case of a spill, an owner or operator might save money by cleaning up what he can by using his own resources. Furthermore, such action might preclude further liability that might otherwise arise from additional pollution damage.

In order to avoid liability for pollution under the act, a charter operator or skipper must prove one or more of the following:

- An act of God;
- An act of war;
- Negligence on the part of the United States government; or
- An act or omission of a third party without regard to whether the act or omission was negligent.

Liability creates a maritime lien against the vessel. The United States is authorized to take action against the vessel and the owner, or both.

Local laws can be tougher. Don't spill and don't let your employees spill. Period.

Actions against the Vessel

A charter operator's boat can be the subject of legal action, such as in the case of a contraband violation. This is called action *in rem*, or action against the thing (the boat), as opposed to action *in personam* (against a person). Seizing a boat and holding it for action *in rem* is much like jailing a person; it ensures that the vessel will be available for a possible sentence. As will be shown, it even allows for the possibility of "bail."

A contraband violation is only one instance of actions *in rem*. Such actions can spring from a variety of maritime liens.[14] A maritime lien is a right of property in the vessel that stays with it wherever she is, until the lien is resolved. If the lien is proven in court, the boat can be sold to satisfy or partially satisfy the lien.[15]

A charter operator who is thinking of buying a vessel should be aware that it could have an unrecorded maritime lien. The best protection against such a possibility, although not guaranteed, is to buy a documented vessel, after obtaining copies of the abstract of title and certificate of ownership from the Coast Guard (as described in the chapter on boat licenses).

Here are some types of maritime liens:

• Crew wages. This lien—which can be placed by master, crew, or any category of employee such as those discussed under the Jones Act—has first priority over all other claims.

• Salvage. This lien can be against the vessel and any cargo saved. A charter operator may subject his vessel to a salvage claim if he and his crew abandon her in the face of a marine peril, and an outside party voluntarily brings her to a safe haven. The operator might also create a salvage claim if his boat is towed when in danger, or under dangerous conditions, even though captain and crew remain aboard.

• Claims for collision, personal injury, and wrongful death under the general maritime law (as opposed to claims under the Jones Act), maintenance and cure, and property damage due to negligence.

• Breach of a charter party, if a charter party has a contract that the owner fails to honor.

• The catchall. The Federal Maritime Lien Act[16] states that any "person furnishing repairs, supplies, towage, use of dry dock or marine railway, or other necessaries, to any vessel . . . shall have a maritime lien on the vessel." The term *other necessaries* has been held by the courts to mean just about anything an operator might buy or order for his boat, such as pilotage, dockage, stevedoring services, marine surveyor fees, a local ship chandler's bill, and costs to clean up and control an oil spill.

How Liens Are Enforced

A lien is foreclosed by a proceeding *in rem*. When the vessel is in the federal district where a verified complaint has been filed, and the district court approves a warrant, a U.S. marshal simply goes out and "arrests" the boat.

The person with the complaint will have to provide an advance deposit to cover insurance costs, as well as custodial keeper costs that will be incurred after its arrest.

As mentioned earlier, except for certain offenses requiring sale of the vessel, the owner can post a bond and recover his vessel. Depending upon the size of the claim, the bond might be higher than the vessel's value. In such a case, if the claimant agrees, the owner can still post a bond for the vessel's value, with stipulations concerning his agreement to pay any additional amount ordered in a final decree.

If the claimant agrees to accept a *letter of undertaking* from the owner, the owner might avoid having to post a bond. This simpler procedure, which can be done even before the vessel is arrested, is a legal guarantee that any judgment up to a specified amount will be paid upon completion of the litigation. A letter of undertaking is somewhat like a person being released on his own recognizance.

If the owner does not claim the vessel and obtain its release, or if the amount of claims outstanding exceeds the value of the vessel, the claimant can ask the court to sell the vessel. Contributing factors here are the costs of keeping the vessel (being paid by the claimant), and whether or not the vessel is deteriorating while under arrest (thus reducing the claimant's chance eventually to receive a full judgment).

If the boat is sold under court order, in a sale confirmed by the court as valid (reasonably advertised, and a bidding procedure designed to bring the best available price), the buyer will receive a lien-free title.

Any charter operator could find himself confronting a lien against his boat. Conversely, his form of charter operation might give cause for him to place a lien against another's boat. In either case, he should pass the facts on to an attorney as fast as a crackle of lightning passes through a stormy anchorage.

Limiting Liability—What a Charter Operator Can Do

As a charter operator, you should discuss the following ideas with an attorney, in order to be sure your business is legally seaworthy:

1. Operate under the Golden Rule of Liability. Keep it uppermost in mind and action. Make sure your employees follow it.

2. Be aware of the Good Samaritan Act. Many states have such an act, which grants immunity from civil liability to a person who gratuitously and in good faith renders emergency care or treatment at the scene of an emergency away from a normal medical treatment site. To be valid, the law generally reads that the person being treated should have no objection, and the person treating should act as an ordinary reasonably prudent person would act under similar circumstances.

3. Be familiar with the Limitation of Liability Act of 1851, which originally was formulated to promote investments in maritime ventures.[17] Under the act, an owner's liability in case of property damage or injury to personnel might be limited to the value of the vessel and its cargo. If the vessel were damaged, his

liability would equal its value after the casualty. The act can also apply to a bareboat charter party as owner. The key qualifying point of the act is whether the owner has "privity or knowledge" of what is happening. If he does, he is still personally liable. This exclusion stems from the reason the act was conceived: A shipowner could hire a master to load his vessel with cargo and deliver it to a foreign port. In case of damage or injuries outside of the owner's privity or knowledge, he should be held liable for no more than his investment (vessel and cargo). A charter operator might more easily prove that he had neither privity nor knowledge if he was not aboard the vessel at the time a casualty occurred. When setting up a charter operation, it is crucial to discuss with an attorney the possible applications of the Limitation of Liability Act.

4. Understand that failure to pay bills connected with your business can earn the boat a maritime lien.

5. Consider your business structure. Incorporation might provide protective insulation.

Summary

1. Legal actions can be taken against an owner, a skipper, or a boat.

2. Liabilities peculiar to charter operations can stem from violation of the Golden Rule of Liability, unseaworthiness, the Jones Act, maintenance and cure actions, death by wrongful act, contraband violations, and pollution.

3. A maritime lien against a boat can result in its being arrested. If a bond or letter of undertaking is not executed, the boat might be sold.

4. By careful planning with your attorney, and adherence to the Golden Rule of Liability, you can minimize your liability. An easy way to remember the Golden Rule is the four Cs: Be careful, conscientious, considerate, and courteous. This will help steer the ship clear of disaster.

CHAPTER 10

Boat Licenses[1]

W ITH few exceptions (such as inner tubes, toy rafts, and some other vessels not equipped with propulsion machinery), there can be no such thing as a boat without a country. Each boat must be sponsored by a political entity, which attests that it is legally owned and is authorized to operate within recognized parameters. Without such sponsorship, no other country would allow it into its waters (or into the waters of its states and cities).

Let's call this sponsorship "licensing," while remembering that we are speaking only of legal permission for a *boat* to be operated. The *operator*, or skipper, of a vessel also might be required to have a license of his own in order to operate the vessel legally (see chapter on captain's licenses and endorsements).

There are three options for licensing a vessel: state numbering, U.S. documentation, and foreign registry. This book only covers numbering and documentation for charter operators. If you are considering foreign registry, you should consult the appropriate country's regulations, or hire an agent.

Numbering in State of Principal Use

Federal law allows states and possessions to create their own numbering systems as long as they meet or exceed federal requirements. Almost all states have such systems. The Coast Guard issues numbers for those states and possessions that don't have them—currently Alaska, New Hampshire, the Northern Marianas, and American Samoa.[2] Unless a charter-boat owner must document, or elects to document (see following section), he has authority to operate his business by numbering the boat in the state of its principal use. If the state has no title law, the owner might obtain a number merely by registering the boat with the state. If the state is one of the twenty-three (as of 1988) with a title law, he can title the boat and get it numbered.

Numbering generally requires proof of ownership, or legal custody, while titling requires a chain of title, proof of ownership, and evidence of liens, or absence of liens in the case of states that issue titles to buyers only after loans have been satisfied. States that impose sales taxes either collect them upon sale or upon registration, or demand proof that an equivalent tax was paid to another state or country. Before you buy—particularly if you do so outside the state where you will do business—be wary of falling into the trap of having to pay a tax twice.

For initial numbering, the location of the *boat* might not matter, since numbering is generally only a matter of filling out the proper forms. However, *the owner* normally must have a mailing address within the state. If the boat was privately built (i.e., has no manufacturer's certificate, or no hull identification number that can be traced over with paper), the state marine patrol agency might insist upon a physical inspection.

Federal Documentation

In 1789, the Congress passed the first discriminatory laws on tonnage dues and customs rates in favor of American vessels. The laws declared that only vessels built in the United States, owned by U.S. citizens, and commanded by American masters could *register* as American vessels. This gave the fledgling U.S. merchant fleet a virtual monopoly of the coastwise trade, and gave the American shipbuilding industry a big boost.

However, our early maritime lawmakers did not give the American shipbuilding industry full carte blanche. For example, if an American captain should capture a European-built or foreign-owned privateer, the Congress felt the vessel should be exempted from the documentation laws. The lawmakers deemed the same in the case of foreign-built ships that might go aground on our shores, and be recovered by Americans. And they included in their exemption foreign-built vessels that our courts might declare forfeited. The Congress empowered the courts to grant these exemptions. The three exceptions to documentation restrictions still remain—under the classifications of wrecked, forfeited, and captured vessels—as will be shown.

The early congressmen also decided that, at any time it would be in the country's best interests to exempt any other non-U.S.-built vessel from the law, they would do so. Thus, today any vessel can be excepted from documentation restrictions by special legislation.

It soon became apparent that our laws were unduly restricting American entrepreneurs from competing in worldwide trade. So, after the War of 1812,

Congress liberalized the *international registry* laws, and permitted our merchantmen to go to and from foreign ports on a reciprocity basis with the countries visited. Congress continued to soften that portion of the laws from time to time, into the twentieth century.

However, the *coastal trade* laws remain ironclad, keeping our fishing industry and coastwise commerce wrapped in a carefully crafted protective shield.

The winds of World War I blew in new reasons to continue coastwise protectionism. As a sea power, we had no intention of becoming impotent, unable to launch a fleet of supply ships in wartime, hence at the mercy of foreign freighters manned by non-American seamen. Our unions agreed, too.

So the protective laws remained. And they continued through World War II, when we supported yet another type of documentation—for pleasure—with the idea that documented pleasure yachts could be requisitioned in wartime for coastal patrol.

But something happened on the way to the twenty-first century. Our merchant fleet began to resemble a phantom. Foreign-flag vessels began hauling more and more of the world's cargo. But they were not exactly foreign vessels. They were owned and operated by American companies that had flagged them to other nations to avoid red tape and increase profits. Today, many American shipping companies explain the situation by asking this rhetorical question: "Why fly the Stars and Stripes, and pay an American a hundred dollars to do a job, if I can flag my ship to another country and pay ten dollars to a worker from a developing country?"

Foreign flagging can increase profits in international commerce, but it seldom fits the needs of a charter operator of smaller vessels. So most charter operators who don't use state numbering will use American documentation laws, as outlined below.

Where Do We Stand Today?

Documentation can be for registry, coastwise license, Great Lakes license, fishery license, pleasure license, or a combination. With certain exceptions, all five forms of documentation require that the owner be a U.S. citizen, and that the vessel be commanded by a U.S. citizen (but see later section in this chapter concerning the word *command*).

Documentation for registry or for pleasure is available to both American-built *and* foreign-built vessels. However, coastwise, Great Lakes, and fishery documentation normally are available only to boats made in the United States.

In addition, coastwise (except coastwise trade in the U.S. Virgin Islands) and Great Lakes documentation are *not* normally available to any vessel that has ever been foreign owned or foreign flagged.

Possible exceptions to the previous two paragraphs are those mentioned earlier: wrecked, forfeited, or captured vessels; and vessels granted coastwise trading privileges by special legislation.

A recent example of special legislation is the Quick Sale Act of 1986, enacted to reduce the glut of boats stored in Florida that had been seized for drug violations. Coast Guard marine safety expert Lieutenant Commander Paul Von Protz says, "If a boat is seized for certain crimes, the government can now sell it after two weeks to the highest bidder." Photos are taken for court use, and the sale proceeds are placed in an interest-bearing escrow account. If the government subsequently loses the case, the money will go to the previous owner of the vessel. Meanwhile, the new owner receives a clear title and can document the boat.

A key exception to the "all-American" rule for coastwise trade concerns charter operators in the U.S. Virgin Islands. Commercial boats operating within the U.S. Virgins *do not* have to be American built, American owned, or American flagged. (All U.S.-documented boats, however, must be under the command of an American citizen.) Hence, an owner of any mechanically propelled vessel operating in the Virgins has three options for flagging: He can number it with the state (Virgin Islands); he can obtain documentation for registry from the Coast Guard; or he can obtain a foreign registry of his choice.

The term *owner* includes an individual, a partnership, an association, a joint venture, a trust, a corporation, or a governmental entity. In multiple ownerships, all principals must be U.S. citizens. In a corporation, this means the chief executive officer, chairman of the board, and a majority of the number of directors necessary to constitute a quorum.

Now for the business of "command." Subchapter G of the Code of Federal Regulations (CFR) 46, which establishes regulations for documentation, states that "No documented vessel shall be commanded by other than a United States citizen."[3] Unfortunately, the CFR doesn't explain what "command" means. The courts have upheld cases wherein the owner (licensed or unlicensed) could hire a licensed non-American captain, as long as he (the owner) remained on board—and in command. The crux of each of these cases seems to depend upon whether the owner could prove to the court that he was competent to handle the boat. This would imply that if he was competent enough to overrule the captain, he was in fact in command.

Types of Documentation for Vessels Over Five Net Tons[4]

1. *Registry* documentation is for foreign trade, which under the law includes trade with Guam, American Samoa, Wake, Midway, and Kingman Reef. Registry does not allow the vessel to fish or conduct trade in the Great Lakes, to fish within the U.S. conservation zone or landward (along our coasts), or to engage in coastwise trade.

2. A *coastwise* license entitles the vessel to employment in coastwise trade and the fisheries. It does not permit the vessel to conduct foreign trade, or Great Lakes coastwise trade or fishing. "Coastwise trade" means that the boat goes no more than twenty miles offshore on an ocean, the Gulf of Mexico, the Caribbean, the Gulf of Alaska, or any other major body of water designated by a Coast Guard district commander. Note that "coastwise" also includes waters adjacent to Puerto Rico and the U.S. Virgin Islands.

3. A *Great Lakes* license entitles the vessel to engage in coastwise trade and the fisheries on the Great Lakes, and to trade with Canada. It does not allow the vessel to conduct foreign trade, or coastwise trade or the fisheries other than in the Great Lakes.

4. A *fishery* license entitles the vessel to conduct commercial fishing under both federal and state fishing laws.

5. A *pleasure* license does not allow the vessel to carry passengers or freight for hire. However, this does not preclude the vessel from being bareboat chartered for pleasure use. Although the boat can be either American or foreign built, it must remain under the command of a U.S. citizen at all times—even when in bareboat charter (see chapter on bareboating).

When Does an Owner Have a Choice of Documentating?

If your boat measures at least five net tons, and does not have to be inspected, and you want to carry on foreign trade, you have the options of either documenting for registry or flagging foreign. If she is at least five net tons, and you want to do bareboat chartering for pleasure, you may either document for pleasure or may obtain a state number. (The phrase *bareboat chartering for pleasure* is used to distinguish such chartering from commercial bareboat chartering. See chapter on bareboating.)

Note that net tons are calculated by a complex measuring system called *admeasurement*. However, you can estimate whether your boat is near five net tons by using a simple formula. First, consider a ton to be equal to about 100 cubic feet of enclosed airspace. The *net* tonnage of a monohull boat would be length times breadth times depth, divided by 100, times .67.[5] For further simplification, a 26-foot monohull boat is often used as an example of five net tons.

Who Must Document in Order to Charter?

You probably need documentation if your boat measures five net tons or more and you intend to charter commercially. (Remember that bareboat chartering for pleasure use is not commercial chartering.) Here is why: "Any vessel of at least 5 net tons which engages in the fisheries, Great Lakes trade, or coastwise trade, unless exempt under 67.01-7, must be documented."[6]

Exempted by 67.01-7 are vessels that do not operate on the navigable waters of the United States; and nonself-propelled vessels legally carrying on coastwise trade within a harbor, on U.S. rivers or inland lakes, or on the internal waters or canals of any state.

The terms *Great Lakes trade* (used by special agreement with Canada) and *coastwise trade* mean carrying either passengers or cargo for hire in and out of U.S. ports.

Navigable waters of the United States[7] means:

• The territorial seas;
• All internal waters subject to tidal influence;
• Other internal waters that have ever been used, or *might* be used for navigation, regardless of man-made obstructions, such as bridges or dams; and
• Waters that a qualified body (governmental or otherwise) determines suitable for conversion to navigation.

Each Coast Guard district keeps a list and charts depicting navigable waters. Write to the district commander to arrange to see a copy, or send him the geographic coordinates of the body of water that concerns your operation. Although the waters listed above might appear to include every last puddle in the country, the Coast Guard can rule (and Congress can declare) a body of water either navigable or nonnavigable.

The Difference Between Documenting and Inspecting

Commander Paul Von Protz explains that vessel licensing regulations (including documentation) control *trade,* and vessel inspection regulations control *safety.* Thus, as we have seen, certain vessels are *eligible* for documentation, and some are *required* to be documented. For safety purposes, whether or not documented, certain vessels must be *inspected.* (See chapter on inspected vessels.)

Remember that virtually anything that floats and is large enough to carry cargo or a passenger is a "vessel." This includes inflatables. Any inflatable over the five-net-ton limit must be documented to be put into charter (except bareboating). And the "American-built" rule still applies. Therefore Zodiac rafts, for example, cannot be used to carry charter passengers because they are made in France.

The Cruise-to-Nowhere Anomaly

The Bureau of Customs has determined that a vessel that goes beyond three miles, stops at no ports, does no fishing, and returns to its original berth is not engaging in coastwise trade. This allows a vessel over five net tons—either documented for registry or foreign flagged—to carry and return passengers. Remember that a vessel that is documented for registry does *not* have to be American built, and a foreign-flagged vessel can be foreign owned and foreign built, and can be commanded by a foreign citizen.

Hence the "voyages-to-nowhere" that some cruise liners make from several American ports. A similar anomaly also occurs with vessels where foreign-built boats are ferrying passengers out to watch whales; and in Florida, where charter operators take passengers out to observe missile launchings.

The "original berth" rule must be observed meticulously. In a classic situation, a cruise ship's berth was occupied temporarily by a damaged vessel. When the cruise liner returned, instead of taking a vacant berth directly astern of the damaged vessel, she stood off for several hours, until she could reclaim her own berth. The skipper was not about to give the Customs Bureau a chance to declare that his vessel was engaging in coastwise trade because it had returned to a different berth.

Penalties

What happens if you don't document when you should? Title 46 U.S. Code, Section 12110(c), essentially says that if you are carrying passengers or cargo in a vessel that is supposed to be documented for that purpose, and it isn't, the U.S. government can seize it and require forfeiture of the vessel and its equipment. Unless you are found innocent in court, the only way you could get your boat back would be to buy it—as the highest bidder at auction. The section also authorizes civil penalties. Vessels involved in any other illegal activities, such as drugs, are also subject to seizure and forfeiture.

How to Document

Every American citizen who owns a qualified boat has the right to document and undocument (take a boat out of documentation) it directly with the Coast Guard. In fact, Part 67 of CFR 46 says that the *owner* must conduct transactions concerning documentation with the Coast Guard.

I have personally documented my last three boats, and I plan to do the same for future ones. Doing the work yourself can save a hefty agent's fee, and it can give you a definite sense of accomplishment. But it can also be frustrating, because, as with other government agencies, the Coast Guard will send the package back if *each* form is not filled out exactly the right way.

So, to save time and heartburn, many charter operators decide to hire an agent to do their documentating. Names of documentation agents can be found in major boating and maritime magazines, in the Yellow Pages for major boating cities, and even at local yacht brokerage offices.

If you decide to document a qualified boat yourself, here is how to do it:

1. Request forms from the nearest Coast Guard documentation office (see Appendix K), with a letter stating:

• Whether this is a request for initial documentation or a request for a change to an existing documentation (specify type of change desired, such as owner change or vessel name change);
• What type or types of documentation are desired;
• Whether the boat is new or used; and
• Whether it is one of the special cases (captured, forfeited, wrecked, or a special-legislation product).

2. Fill out the forms and provide other information exactly as requested. For a summary of forms, and the information you will be expected to provide, see Appendix E.

Markings Required on Documented Boats

A documented vessel must be marked on the stern with its name and hailing port.[8] If the boat is documented commercially, the name must also be on both bows. All markings must be at least four inches high. In addition, the official number (ON) must be permanently marked on some clearly visible interior structural part of the hull. (This is a change from a former requirement that the ON be marked on the main beam.)

Home Ports and Hailing Ports

The hailing port marked on the boat generally is the city and state of the owner's legal address, if in the United States. If the owner's legal address is outside the United States, it is the same city as the home port. It cannot be a foreign city.

The home port is what the Coast Guard calls the *port of documentation*—the city where the documentation office that keeps the boat's records is located.

An owner living overseas, with a legal address in the United States, uses the same hailing port and home port as if living at the U.S. address. An owner living overseas with no legal U.S. address may contact any documentation office and will use that office address as both hailing and home port.

Special Advice Concerning Coast Guard Bills of Sale

The Coast Guard uses its own bill-of-sale form merely as proof of ownership. It doesn't care what price was paid for the boat. Although it will accept a phrase such as "ten dollars and other considerations" as the purchase price, this does not relieve the buyer of paying a state tax. Owners of documented vessels have recently found out the hard way that the states are collecting tax money by obtaining Coast Guard records of documentation under the Freedom of Information Act, and tracing down the owners for delinquent taxes.

Advantages and Disadvantages of Documentation

If you have a choice whether to number or document, your selection of one over the other will depend upon how it affects the ease and cost of doing business. The comments that follow might help you decide.

Prior to 1963, state titling laws were unheard of, and documentation was the only practical way to get a loan to purchase a large boat. Documentation made the vessel the subject of a preferred ship mortgage under the Ship Mortgage Act of 1920. Today your lender still might insist upon documentation, but more and more states are turning to boat titling laws that include reciprocity. And more and more charter operators are simply buying and financing their boats just like they buy and finance automobiles—through their state systems. If you will be doing business in a title state, documentation may offer no advantage when applying for a loan. Check with your lender.

However, watch out for the unexpected. American Airlines captain J. W. ("Bill") Kingsley bought a state-numbered Ericson 35 on Lake Texoma, on the Texas-Oklahoma border, and had no problem with a loan. A year later, he notified the bank that he was thinking of removing the boat from the lake, only to be told, "Not unless you document it." The loan officer didn't want the boat out sailing the seven seas without a certificate of documentation showing the bank as lienholder.

Also, think ahead to the day you will want to sell. Will the prospective buyer, *and his lender,* want a documented boat? Conversely, does your sales market include a high percentage of foreigners, who cannot own a documented vessel?

Now for two tales that seem to hang around like a welcoming committee on the docks. First, it has been said that a certificate of documentation may simplify customs and immigration formalities in foreign ports. However, none of the almost three hundred charter operators queried for this book provided an example to support this.

Second, it has been said that a certificate of documentation makes a boat an extension of the U.S. government, and that, should the boat be confiscated by a foreign power, the Great White Fleet will come to its rescue. Well, the Great White Fleet had its hulls painted gray long ago. If the government should contemplate sending a gray-hulled battle group to rescue an American charter boat today, the ultimate decision would probably have little to do with whether the boat was documented or state-numbered.

What Are the Costs?

Initial documentation for pleasure is currently $51 or more, plus a fee for an agent if you use one. For bareboating, this might be more expensive than state-numbering your boat. On the other hand, if you document your vessel for other than pleasure, there is no initial charge. Here is a sample of fees[9] charged by the Coast Guard:

Change vessel name	$100.00
Change home port, ownership, etc.	50.00
Replace lost document	50.00
Record bill of sale	1.00 each
Annual renewal	no charge

Except for the recording of bills of sale, the Coast Guard fees are not cumulative. In multiple transactions, only the highest fee is charged. For example, to change the name of a vessel, change the home port, *and* replace a lost document, the fee would be $100.

To change ownership and home port of a documented vessel when there were two previous owners, the fee would be $52 ($50 plus $2 to record the two original bills of sale). The only fees applicable to a commercial vessel are those for recording bills of sale and changes of vessel names.

Summary

1. Boat licenses should not be confused with operator licenses, which are covered in another chapter.

2. Boat licensing must be by state numbering, U.S. documentation, or foreign registry. You may have a choice, but if the boat you put into charter service is over five net tons and will be on navigable U.S. waters, you probably must document.

3. General Documentation Requirements

	American Built?	Owner American?	Commanded by American?	Mandatory if 5 NT
Registry	no	yes	yes	no
Coastwise[a]	yes	yes	yes	yes
Great Lakes[a]	yes	yes	yes	yes
Fishery	yes	yes	yes	yes
Pleasure	no	yes	yes	no

Note a. Coastwise and Great Lakes documentation not available if vessel was *ever* owned by a non-U.S. citizen or *ever* foreign flagged.

4. Some exceptions to general documentation requirements: bareboats, voyages-to-nowhere, U.S. Virgin Islands.

5. "Navigable waters of the United States": Most waters are navigable. Coast Guard district offices have lists and charts. Determinations of navigability can be changed.

6. How to document: (a) Obtain forms and instructions from Coast Guard documentation office; and (b) Use chapter information and appendices; or (c) Hire an agent.

CHAPTER 11

Inspected Vessels—What Makes Them Different?

THE requirement for inspection of what the Coast Guard calls "small passenger vessels (under 100 gross tons)" stems from the Coast Guard's mandate to ensure minimum safety standards for commercial vessels. The regulations, codified in 46 CFR 166-199, are often modified.[1] Coast Guard marine safety expert Lieutenant Commander Paul R. Von Protz explains, "The regulations are continually being rewritten due to lessons learned through casualties. When a casualty occurs, we want to find out why, so we can possibly prevent a similar one in the future. That's why we say that the regulations are 'written in blood.'"

Which Vessels Must Be Inspected?[2]

Unless a boat operates exclusively upon waters that have been declared nonnavigable (see chapter on boat licenses), it must be *inspected* if it weighs:

- Over one hundred gross tons and carries one or more passengers;
- One hundred gross tons or less and carries seven or more passengers;

or

- Fifteen gross tons or more and carries cargo.

Because charter operators seldom use boats that are over one hundred gross tons, requirements for vessels in that category are not covered in this book.

Exceptions

A foreign-flagged vessel that does not engage in coastwise trade is not required to be inspected if its country of registry is a signatory of SOLAS (Safety of Life at Sea, an international convention). However, it is subject to verification that the country of registry has carried out an inspection.

What Constitutes an "Inspection"?

Inspection, for which the owner deals with the Coast Guard's inspection department, is a separate process from documentation. Inspection is *not* the same as a Coast Guard Auxiliary courtesy inspection, or a Coast Guard boarding inspection. It is a detailed study that a Coast Guard marine inspection officer makes of the boat's construction and its passenger safety devices and facilities to ensure that they meet the exacting written standards contained in the Code of Federal Regulations.

The marine inspection officers operate from marine safety offices (MSO), marine inspection offices (MIO), marine safety detachments (MSD), and marine inspection detachments (MID). (Subsequent references in this chapter to these organizations are indicated by "MSO/MIO.")

Charter boat owners involved in boat inspection should contact the MSO/MIO nearest to the boat's location. If the boat will be operating in an area outside the MSO/MIO's jurisdiction, the owner should also contact the appropriate MSO/MIO for that operating area. (For addresses of MSO/MIOs, see Appendix K.)

If the inspection of a small passenger vessel (less than one hundred gross tons) is satisfactory, the owner will receive a certificate of inspection (Coast Guard Form 3753), which will describe:

the vessel, the route which she may travel, the minimum manning requirements, the major lifesaving equipment carried, the minimum fire extinguishing equipment and life preservers required to be carried, the maximum number of passengers and the maximum number of persons which may be carried, the name of the owner and operator, and such conditions of operations as may be determined by the Officer in Charge, Marine Inspection.[3]

The owner must place this certificate under glass or other transparent material, in a prominent place, unless such posting would be impracticable. In such a case, he must keep it on board to be shown on demand.[4]

With the certificate of inspection comes the requirement to carry out a host of regulations pertaining to inspected vessels. Of prime importance, the owner or captain must:

1. Provide a safety orientation for passengers;

2. Post an emergency check-off list in a conspicuous place that is accessible to the crew and passengers; and

3. Have available a life preserver for every person on board.

Along with the certificate of inspection, the owner receives a sticker showing that the boat has been inspected and the date the certificate expires. The sticker is posted where passengers can see it when boarding.

Certification—How to Get an Inspection Certificate

In a questionnaire mailed to experts in all phases of chartering operations, I asked what advice captains had about vessel inspection and certification. One swashbuckling old captain replied simply, "Hide!"

He was complaining about the seemingly endless chain of delays that sometimes occur en route to that certification. In his years of experience, he had learned that the Coast Guard, with some 40,000 active-duty members and 6,000 civilians, is a bureaucracy that behaves like all bureaucracies do at times—slowly, sometimes erratically, and often incomprehensibly.

Naturally, anyone going into business with a boat that needs to be inspected wants to get that boat on the water immediately. But it's worth moving carefully in the beginning to establish the chartering operation that you are likely to live with for a long time.

Below are listed seven possible courses you might take to save time, temper, and money. In each case, contact the MSO/MIO handling the vessel, and consider hiring an agent who knows the marine inspection business.

1. Buy a new boat with an inspection certificate affixed. This can be relatively simple, depending upon the type of charter operation you are considering. For instance, Delta Boat Works in Cape Canaveral, Florida, advertises 38-foot dive boats that are Coast Guard-certified to carry twenty-eight passengers for hire. South Seas Catamaran, Inc., in Fort Myers, Florida, offers a similar package, with a 43-foot dive boat designed for sixty-nine passengers.

2. Buy a used boat that has already been inspected. You can apply for a renewal certificate, thus making sure the vessel still fits the Coast Guard criteria, before you close the deal. Be aware, however, that if the boat is certified within the jurisdiction of an MSO/MIO different from yours, the inspection must be transferred to yours.

3. Order a sistership to a boat that has already been certified.

4. Build a boat similar to an existing certified boat, in order to take advantage of construction techniques already accepted by the MSO/MIO. For example, more excursion submarines probably will be built because of the certification of the small passenger-carrying submarine *Atlantis III* in 1987. If a company can build a submarine with expectation of successful certification, you should be able to clone a surface craft!

5. Discover what inspected boats your nearest MSO/MIO controls, find one you like, *then* find a sistership for sale. Plan to have her inspected at the same MSO/MIO.

6. Build a new model to fit your chartering needs, in close coordination with your naval architect, the builder, and the MSO/MIO.

7. Convert a boat. This can be a wrenching, costly project if not planned and carried out carefully. Get the best possible advice from real experts in advance: naval architects, builders, and marine inspectors from the MSO/MIO. A few dollars on the front end might save you thousands later. For instance, adding rails around your decks alone might mean a major modification of gunwale, decking, and hull. Then there might be retrofits involving rewiring, installation of collision bulkheads, new plumbing, and a dozen or more other projects, as shown in Appendix H.

If you elect to go with an inspected boat, and you have located one or have decided to build one, immediately contact the MSO/MIO nearest to the boat's location. If the boat will operate in *another* MSO/MIO jurisdiction, contact that organization also. Prior to the start of construction (or before the initial inspection, if it is a used boat), the marine inspector will need detailed copies of the plans—*detailed*. He will tell you exactly what he wants, and probably will provide information on how to prepare your input. If there is a sistership, with plans already in the hands of the MSO, he might not ask for another set.

A word of caution. If you have a boat that has never been inspected for certification, study Appendix H. A few hours on the boat with the checklist should give you a good idea of what will have to be done. You'll find that some of the requirements on the checklist are also suitable advice for an uninspected boat—such as removing all dead and unused wire. If the terminology in the appendix seems vague, you might want to think twice about operating an inspected boat, or at least consider hiring a hot-shot engineer with proven experience in Coast Guard marine inspections to assist.

What Is an Uninspected Vessel?[5]

Any boat used to carry passengers or cargo for hire that is not required to be inspected automatically earns the title "uninspected vessel." This doesn't exclude it, however, from the watchful eyes of the Coast Guard. Uninspected vessels fall under their own set of regulations, beginning with a maximum passenger load of six (hence the term *six-pack*). *Do not forget* that rule. If a boat is not inspected, it cannot legally carry more than six passengers for hire.

The Coast Guard enforces safety regulations for uninspected vessels by courtesy inspections, by random boardings, or by boardings as a result of casualty. For safety requirements for uninspected vessels, see Subchapter C of 46 CFR, Parts 1-40. Appendix G has information for ordering 46 CFR, Parts 1-40, from the Government Printing Office. Some Coast Guard license prep schools offer copies for sale. Also, the nearest MSO/MIO will have a copy you can examine, as will many large libraries.

Summary

1. Vessels of less than one hundred gross tons carrying more than six passengers for hire must be inspected. (However, see chapter on bareboating for determination of number of guests.)

2. Any boat carrying passengers or cargo for hire that is not required to be inspected is regulated under the rules for "uninspected vessels."

3. Uninspected vessels are often called "six-packs" because they can take no more than six passengers for hire.

4. Doing careful homework before starting the inspection procedure can save time, money, and good dispositions.

5. Appendix H gives a summary of what it might take to convert a pleasure boat for certification.

CHAPTER 12

Captain's Licenses and Endorsements

W HO needs a license? Anybody putting a boat with a motor on it into chartering service who expects to operate it on navigable waters needs a license, if (1) he expects to carry one or more passengers for hire, or (2) he plans to operate the boat other than for pleasure.[1]

What Is a Passenger for Hire?

The regulations for uninspected vessels and for inspected vessels to one hundred gross tons both state that carrying passengers for hire means: "The carriage of any person or persons by a vessel for a valuable consideration, whether directly or indirectly flowing to the owner, charterer, operator, agent or any other person interested in the vessel."[2]

To be carrying passengers for hire, the skipper doesn't have to stand at the boarding ladder collecting tickets. If money, or something that passes for money, changes hands at any phase of his chartering business, and the customer takes a ride on his boat, the captain probably ought to be licensed.

First there is an example of a dive-shop operator. Six people paid Joe Divemaster to teach them how to dive. He explained that his fee covered the classroom and swimming pool sessions. As a "bonus," or "discount," he would transport them to their end-of-course open-water dive sites by boat, at no charge. There was a profit motive, and money had changed hands. He was carrying passengers for hire.

Once upon a time, a sailing-school operator tried another angle. A student signed on with the school to learn to sail on a boat equipped with an auxiliary engine. During the practical application periods, his teacher—who was employed by the school as a "classroom instructor"—accompanied him. The instructor's contract with the school forbade him from touching the rigging or the helm. Never mind. Whether or not he touched the rigging or the helm, he was carrying a passenger for hire.

112

Ski boats need licensed operators to tow customers in navigable waters—which means along saltwater beaches, in rivers, or on most streams and lakes. And so do parasail boats, and boats that tow or launch hang gliders. Also, if customers are ferried to or lifted from a parasail barge, or a hang glider barge, the ferry operator and the barge operator must be licensed. (And if the ferry operator takes a second group of six passengers to the barge without returning the first six, the barge must be inspected.)

The same rules apply to fishing guides and hunting guides, harbor excursion-vessel operators, airboat tour guides, and glass-bottomed boat operators—any time they operate on navigable waters.

The requirement holds whether a boat is under way or at anchor. For example, a dive-boat operator with divers in the water must keep a licensed operator on board at all times. If the boat is anchored and the skipper wants to attend the dive, he'd better leave another licensed operator on board.

Why? The answer comes in two steps. First, the regulations require that the operator of a boat carrying passengers for hire be licensed. This is a means of creating a minimum level of safety protection for the passengers. Second, even though the passengers may be diving, a licensed operator on board ensures that there will be a safe boat for their return. The operator can monitor the weather, take steps to prevent or stop dragging, discover and suppress fire or flooding, and do all the other things he would do for safety when the passengers are aboard.

When Is a Boat Operated Not for Pleasure?

If the regulations concerning passengers for hire don't convince a charter operator that he needs a license, Public Law 98-89, passed in 1983, certainly might. Under the law, an owner or a person operating for the owner must be licensed to carry passengers even if he receives no money or other valuable consideration—unless he is operating the boat only for pleasure.

Under this law, you can be deemed to be operating not for pleasure if you take a group of media representatives for a spin around the lake, or even if you ferry your church group from point A to point B. If it's not for pleasure, it requires a license.

If you believe you have figured out a watertight plan to avoid obtaining a captain's license, you might get an opinion about it from the Coast Guard. Although they have rejected almost every plan devised to avoid using licensed operators, perhaps yours will fit within the law as neatly as a well-folded sail fits into its bag. After all, private charter operators didn't try bareboat demise chartering for pleasure until after World War II (see chapter on bareboating).

But you are in business to make profits, and net profits suffer when the overhead rises, whether it be from debt service or legal costs. So be careful about tying your operation into a legal knot that lies lazy in the stern, ready to fall off and foul your prop just when you're well under way. If your plan could cost you more money in the courts than it is likely to return in profits, it might be simpler to get a license, or hire employees with licenses.

Becoming a Captain—The Licenses

The type of license needed to operate a charter boat[3] depends upon three factors:

1. Whether the vessel is inspected or uninspected;
2. Whether it will operate solely upon Great Lakes/inland waters, or will also operate on other than inland waters; and
3. Its tonnage.

In an effort to simplify the subject, this chapter treats uninspected vessels and inspected vessels as separate groups. Licenses and endorsements for different operating areas are discussed within the subdivisions of each group. Licenses as master or mate (rivers) are not discussed, as service requirements for these licenses are the same as for inland licenses. Tonnage requirements are included where relevant. But first some basics.

The Difference Between Inland and "Other Than Inland" Waters

Prior to December 1, 1987, inland waters stopped at the head of each bay or inlet, as declared by the local officer in charge of marine inspection (OCMI). On December 1, 1987, the licensing system underwent major modifications. Inland waters now stop at the *boundary line*.[4]

Once seaward of the boundary line, you are in "other than inland" waters. All waters seaward of the boundary line are called "ocean" or "oceans." The first two hundred miles offshore is "near coastal."[5]

The definitions for these terms will be important when reading the requirements for the licenses. (The following abbreviations are used: Great Lakes = GL; Inland = IN; Near coastal = NC.)

Requirements for All Licenses to 200 Tons[6]

Twelve basic requirements must be met in order to attain any license.

1. Minimum age. Based upon type of license.
2. Qualifying time. Have a minimum amount of experience on the water, based upon type of license. Although most of this can be accumulated during a lifetime, at least ninety days must have been in the previous thirty-six months.

Time employed in deck service counts. Time aboard a noncrewed charter boat counts. And time aboard a crewed charter boat might count also—if the owner or skipper certifies that you weren't acting like a passenger on the *QE 2*.

Qualifying time can be on boats used strictly for pleasure, with eight hours counting as a day. Some regional exam centers (RECs) allow four hours to count as a day on vessels under one hundred gross tons. On commercial boats, eight hours may count as a day, and twelve as a day-and-a-half, depending upon the watch system. Policies can vary from one REC to another.[7] (Seé Appendix K for addresses of RECs.) Check with either the nearest REC or a knowledgeable license prep organization.

Living aboard—at a pier, on a mooring, or at anchor—does not normally count as qualifying time. Nor does time as a paying, nonworking, passenger aboard a dive boat, a head boat, a party boat, or the *QE 2*.

If during a "day" on the water you cross the COLREGS demarcation line (marking where the International Rules of the Road apply), that day counts as a qualifying day on ocean or near-coastal waters.

If you are an owner of a boat under two hundred gross tons, you can attest to your own service. If your qualifying time is noncommercial on somebody else's boat, a letter from the owner is normally required, although the REC might accept a letter from a marina operator, or anybody else who should know. If your time is commercial, you will need letters, discharges, or other acceptable documents from owners or licensed persons. For sea service as a member of the armed forces, you will need an official transcript.

The Coast Guard will accept reasonable equivalence to the required qualifying time. Peter Kreuziger, originally from Austria, can attest to this. Peter is co-owner of *U.S. Bon Appetit,* a 61-foot luxury vessel in Florida that is also a five-star floating restaurant. Imagine submitting a form attesting to so many days on the Danube, so many on alpine lakes, so many more on various European rivers. The Coast Guard bought it, and Kreuziger is now a licensed captain.

The Coast Guard has approved some training courses, including simulator training, that might be acceptable for part of the qualifying time. The nearest REC can advise further on this.

3. Physical exam. Your physician, or physician's assistant, must certify the following in writing, which can be done on a standard Coast Guard form (CG-719K):

a. That your general physical condition does not indicate epilepsy, insanity, senility, acute general disease or neurosyphilis, badly impaired hearing, or any other defect that would render you incompetent to perform the ordinary duties that your license would entail.

b. That you have uncorrected vision of at least 20/200 in each eye, correctable to at least 20/40 in each eye.

c. That your color sense is satisfactory when tested by any of the following: Pseudo-isochromatic Plates; Eldridge Green Color Perception Lantern; Farnsworth Lantern; Keystone Orthoscope; Keystone Tele-binocular; SAMCTT; Titmus Optical Vision Tester; or Williams Lantern. (Your examiner will understand these tests, and will certify on the form the test he uses.)

If a physical deficiency exists, the case can be sent to the commandant of the Coast Guard for a second opinion. The key here is first to convince the OCMI that extenuating circumstances exist. Recommendations from owners and skippers concerning your proven abilities can help. Even color blindness is not an absolute bar to a license, because it is possible to obtain a license restricted to daytime use.

4. Proof of U.S. citizenship. Required for all vessels except uninspected, undocumented vessels.

5. English. Have the ability to speak and understand English. (For Puerto Rico exception, see next section.)

6. First aid. Have completed a first-aid course within the previous twelve months from the American Red Cross, a Coast Guard–approved school, or a school the OCMI determines exceeds the standards of the Red Cross course.

7. CPR. Have a currently valid certificate of completion of a CPR course from the American Red Cross, the American Heart Association, or a Coast Guard–approved school.

8. Character references. Obtain recommendations from three persons who have knowledge of your suitability for duty. If your qualifying time derives from pleasure cruises, the recommendations can be from anybody who knows you. If your qualifying time is commercial, the recommendations must be from licensed officers, one of whom must be a master.

9. No recent narcotics violations. Have not been convicted of a violation of the narcotic drug laws of the United States, the District of Columbia, or any state or territory of the United States, within three years prior to date of filing the application (ten years if the gravity of the facts or circumstances warrant).

10. No drug addiction. Have never been the user of or addicted to the use of a narcotic drug, unless you furnish satisfactory evidence that you are "cured."

11. Fingerprints. Submit fingerprint forms at time of application. These will be sent to the FBI. If through fingerprinting or any other source the OCMI receives information indicating that your habits of life and character warrant the belief that you cannot be entrusted with the duties and responsibilities of the license you are applying for, your application may be rejected. You may appeal such a rejection.

12. Written exam. This will be covered in detail in a following section.

Operator of Uninspected Passenger Vessels— The Six-Pack[8]

The OUPV, or six-pack license (formerly "motorboat operator" license), is a special license used to carry six passengers or fewer for hire on uninspected vessels. Note the term *uninspected*. A six-pack operator can carry passengers for hire *only* on uninspected boats. He cannot legally operate an inspected vessel, even if it is carrying six or fewer passengers.

The license is valid on uninspected vessels of less than one hundred gross tons that are equipped with any type of propulsion machinery. This includes sailboats with auxiliary engines or motors. (Uninspected sailboats of less than one hundred tons with *no* auxiliary power do not require the operators to be licensed.) The requirements (in addition to the requirements for *all* licenses) are:

1. The minimum age is eighteen.

2. Qualifying time is 360 days. For the near-coastal-waters endorsement (not more than one hundred miles offshore for six-pack operators), at least ninety days must be on ocean or near-coastal waters.

3. All applicants must be able to speak, read, and understand English, except for Spanish-speaking applicants who intend to operate in the vicinity of Puerto Rico, who may apply for a license restricted to that area.

The six-pack license is the only U.S. license a non-U.S. citizen can hold. It does *not* authorize a noncitizen to operate a documented vessel. Remember that no six-pack operator can legally command an *inspected* vessel.

Licenses for Inspected Vessels—General[9]

Inspected passenger vessels of under one hundred gross tons have a special set of regulations called "Subchapter T" of the Code of Federal Regulations (CFR). (This is why they are often called "T-boats.") Licenses to operate T-boats are issued in fifty-gross-ton increments based on the applicant's qualifying experience. An exception is an applicant whose entire qualifying service was aboard boats of five tons or less; his endorsement would be for twenty-five tons. Even though an inspected-vessel license might limit the holder to *inspected* vessels of fifty tons or less, his license authorizes him to operate an *uninspected* vessel (six-pack) of up to one hundred tons within the geographical limitations of his license.

In addition to T-boat licenses, the sections that follow also outline the requirements for the two types of licenses of under two hundred tons that are most likely to be used by charter operators. If the individual meets qualifying-time requirements for these larger licenses, and passes the additional examination topics specified in Appendix F, he can serve on vessels of up to two hundred tons.

Licenses for inspected vessels are issued only to U.S. citizens, with some exceptions. For instance, passenger-carrying submarines in the U.S. Virgin Islands can be commanded by noncitizens with "letters of competence," as can other inspected vessels in those waters.

Great Lakes and Inland Licenses for
Inspected Vessels

A license for IN can be used for all inland waters except the Great Lakes. A license for GL/IN can be used for both Great Lakes and inland waters. A Great Lakes endorsement on an inland license requires at least three months of service on the Great Lakes. Because inland waters sometimes extend beyond the COLREGS demarcation line, an applicant for a GL/IN or IN license must complete an examination on the COLREGS (the International Rules of the

Road) or the license will be endorsed to exclude waters beyond the COLREGS line.

Master (Great Lakes or Inland), 25 to 100 Gross Tons

A "Master (GL/IN) 25-100 GT" can serve on an inspected vessel (GL/IN) within the tonnage limitations of his license. He can also command an uninspected vessel (six-pack) to one hundred gross tons. Requirements (in addition to the requirements for *all* licenses) are:

1. The minimum age is nineteen.
2. Qualifying time is 360 days of service on any waters.
3. For a sail or auxiliary sail endorsement, the applicant must have served 180 days at any time aboard the respective type of vessel.

Inland Operator

The last "Inland Operator" licenses, which authorize the holders to operate inspected vessels (GL/IN) within route and tonnage limitations, were issued on November 30, 1987. On the following day, December 1, existing inland operator licenses became the equivalents of "Master (GL/IN) 25-100 GT" when endorsed accordingly. (Endorsements depend upon the holder's qualifications.) The last inland operator licenses expire in 1992.

Mate (Great Lakes and Inland), 25 to 200 Gross Tons

A "Mate (GL/IN) 25-200 GT" can serve as a mate on an inspected vessel (GL/IN) within the tonnage limitations on his license. He cannot command an inspected vessel or an uninspected boat (six-pack). Requirements (in addition to those for *all* licenses) are:

1. The minimum age is eighteen.
2. Qualifying time is 180 days of service in the deck department of steam, motor, sail, or auxiliary sail vessels (i.e., vessels of any propulsion) in any navigable waters.
3. For a sail or auxiliary sail endorsement, the applicant must have served ninety days at any time aboard the respective type of vessel.
4. A master of steam or motor vessels with ninety days of service aboard a sail or auxiliary sail vessel may get a mate's endorsement (GL/IN) for the respective type of vessel.

5. An OUPV (GL/IN) (six-pack operator) may get an endorsement for mate (GL/IN) by completing a limited examination.

Master (Great Lakes or Inland), 25 to 200 Gross Tons

A "Master (GL/IN) 25-200 GT" can serve on an inspected vessel (GL/IN) within the tonnage limitations of his license. He can also command an uninspected vessel (six-pack) (GL/IN) to one hundred gross tons. Requirements (in addition to the requirements for *all* licenses) are:

1. The minimum age is nineteen.
2. Qualifying time is 360 days of service on vessels, 180 days of which must have been as master, mate, or equivalent supervisory position while holding a license as master, mate, operator, or second-class operator of uninspected towing vessels, or OUPV (six-pack operator).
3. For a sail or auxiliary sail endorsement, the applicant must have served 180 days at any time aboard the respective type of vessel.

Near-Coastal Licenses for Inspected Vessels

Master (Near Coastal), 25 to 100 Gross Tons

A "Master (NC) 25-100 GT" can command an inspected vessel within the tonnage limitations of his license. He can also command an uninspected vessel (six-pack) to one hundred gross tons. Requirements (in addition to the requirements for *all* licenses) are:

1. The minimum age is nineteen.
2. Qualifying time is 720 days of deck service, at least 360 days of which must have been on ocean or near-coastal routes.
3. For a sail or auxiliary sail endorsement, the applicant must have served 360 days at any time aboard the respective type of vessel.

Ocean Operator

The last "Ocean Operator" licenses, which authorize the holders to operate inspected vessels within route and tonnage limitations, were issued on November 30, 1987. On the following day, December 1, existing ocean operator licenses became the equivalents of "Master (NC) 100 GT" when endorsed accordingly. (Endorsements depend upon the holder's qualifications.) The last ocean operator licenses expire in 1992.

Mate (Near Coastal), 25 to 200 Gross Tons

A "Mate (NC) 25-200 GT" can serve as a mate on an inspected vessel within the tonnage limitations of his license, and can command an uninspected vessel (six-pack) to one hundred gross tons. Requirements, in addition to the requirements for *all* licenses, are:

1. The minimum age is eighteen.

2. Qualifying time is 360 days of service in the deck department on vessels of any propulsion, at least 180 days of which must have been on ocean or near-coastal waters.

3. Qualifying time for a master (IN), any propulsion, is ninety days of service in the deck department of steam or motor vessels operating on ocean or near-coastal waters.

4. For a sail or auxiliary sail endorsement, the applicant must have served 180 days at any time aboard the respective type of vessel.

5. A master of steam or motor vessels with ninety days of service aboard a sail or auxiliary sail vessel may get an endorsement for the respective type of vessel.

6. An OUPV/NC (six-pack operator) may get an endorsement for mate (NC) by completing a limited examination.

Master (Near Coastal), 25 to 200 Gross Tons

A "Master (NC) 25-200 GT" can command an inspected vessel within the tonnage limitations of his license. He can also command an uninspected vessel (six-pack) to one hundred gross tons. Requirements (in addition to the requirements for *all* licenses) are:

1. The minimum age is nineteen.

2. Qualifying time is 720 days of service, of which at least 360 days must have been as master, mate, or equivalent supervisory position while holding a license as master, mate, or OUPV (six-pack operator). At least 360 days of the qualifying time must have been on ocean or near-coastal waters; or 360 days of total service as a licensed operator or second-class operator of ocean or near-coastal uninspected towing vessels.

3. For a sail or auxiliary sail endorsement, the applicant must have served 360 days at any time aboard the respective type of vessel.

Captains, Heed This

No matter which license is involved, the maximum number of passengers is limited in every case by the license itself or the type of boat, or both. Because of this, any captain in the chartering business should be certain he knows *exactly* how to count passengers. Below is an explanation of how the Coast Guard does it.

What Is a Passenger?

The regulations for uninspected vessels and inspected vessels state:

> A passenger is every person, other than the master and the members of the crew or other persons employed or engaged in any capacity on board a vessel in the business of that vessel. In the case of a vessel on an international voyage a child under one year of age is not counted as a passenger.[10]

For inspected vessels, the regulations add:

> The term *passenger* means every person carried on board a vessel other than:

1. The owner or his representative;
2. The master and the bona fide members of the crew engaged in the business of the vessel who have contributed no consideration for their carriage and who are paid for their services;
3. Any employee of the owner of the vessel engaged in the business of the owner, except when the vessel is operating under a bareboat charter;
4. Any employee of the bareboat charterer of the vessel engaged in the business of the bareboat charterer;
5. Any guest on board a vessel which is being used exclusively for pleasure purposes who has not contributed any consideration directly or indirectly for his carriage; or
6. Any person on board a vessel documented and used for tugboat or towboat service of fifty gross tons or more who has not contributed any consideration, directly or indirectly, for his carriage.[11]

Requirements for Licenses in Foreign Countries

If the boat is flagged in the United States and is to be used commercially anywhere in the world, the owner must comply with U.S. law regarding inspection, documentation, and licensing. Coast Guard marine-safety specialist Lieutenant Commander Paul Von Protz explains:

> If the captain carries six passengers for hire up and down the Seine River, he must be properly licensed. If he carries more than six passengers, the vessel must have a valid certificate of inspection, and he must be licensed accordingly. If he wishes to carry cargo, and the vessel is over fifteen tons, it also must carry a valid certificate of inspection. If he carries *any* passengers, and the vessel is over one hundred tons, it must have a certificate . . .

If the vessel carries commercial cargo, such as cheese, up and down the Meuse River in Holland, the vessel must be under control of a licensed operator. If it is U.S. documented, the operator must be a U.S. citizen. If it is state numbered, the operator may be a noncitizen, but he must have an equivalent foreign license that is recognized by the United States.

The United States recognizes equivalent licenses issued by countries that are members of SOLAS (Safety of Life at Sea, an international convention) that provide reciprocity.

The Written Exam

The Coast Guard conducts and monitors the written exam, which is multiple choice. Although there is no time limit (as of this writing), it must be completed in one sitting. Most applicants finish within four to six hours. If you finish early, it would be foolish to leave without reviewing every question and checking every calculation.

Although the questions are not supposed to be misleading, they *can* be difficult. The section on the Rules of the Road is the most exacting, because the Coast Guard sets 90 percent as a passing grade for this section. A grade of 70 percent will do for the other sections, but check with the REC, or a license prep school, for your specific exam.

You must pass every section of the exam to get your license. If you fail three or more sections, you will have to take and pass a complete reexamination. If you fail three or more sections the second time, you will be required to wait (i.e., study) three months before trying again.

If you fail one or two sections, you can retake them—up to twice within the following three months. If you haven't passed all sections by then, you will be required to wait three months before trying again . . . and will have to take the entire examination at that time.

The Coast Guard estimates that 10,000 people take basic exams each year—and only 60 percent pass. To stack the deck in your favor, you should be properly prepared.

Preparing For the Exam

There are three ways to prepare for the examination: studying reference materials, using a home-study prep course, or attending a license prep school course.

Studying the References. Applicants with a broad base of experience and a good educational background often use this method of preparation. You should be able to schedule study periods and stick to the schedule. You will need to create a study program for yourself, just as a teacher creates a syllabus for students. You should match the reference materials against the subjects the Coast Guard expects you to know (see Appendix F); organize each subject into logical components; develop learning aids for retention; discover your weaknesses and find ways to overcome them. If you have already taken a U.S. Power Squadron course, or a Coast Guard Auxiliary course, you'll have a leg up. If you haven't, you probably will want to concentrate strictly on your study program. This method of preparation can cost less than the other two methods if you already have the reference materials or can borrow them. Here are examples of some of the references you might need (also see Bibliography):

- *Chapman's Piloting, Seamanship and Small Boat Handling.*
- *The Ship's Medicine Chest and First Aid at Sea.*
- *Light List, List of Lights, Radio Navigational Aids, Coast Pilot, Sailing Directions, Tide Tables, Tidal Current Tables*, and Nautical Chart No. 1.
- Kotsch: *Weather for the Mariner.*
- Maritime Administration: *Marine Fire Prevention, Firefighting, and Fire Safety.*

- IALA buoyage system pamphlet.
- *Watchkeeping For Seafarers* (STCW), 1978
- USCG Publication COMDTINST M 16759.4b: *Boating Safety Train-ing Manual.*
- *International Regulations for Preventing Collisions at Sea, 1972*, and *Inland Navigation Rules* (Rules of the Road).
- U.S. Code of Federal Regulations: Titles 33 and 46.

If you know *everything* in the references, you will be as savvy as Captain Horatio Hornblower. But the scope of information in *Chapman* alone can be for-midable—and often peripheral to the mission at hand, which is to answer correctly the specific questions on the exam.

You must be able to convert your knowledge into answers that the Coast Guard will accept. For some questions, two possible choices seem equally correct. For others, *no* answer looks right. This is why even Horatio Hornblower might opt for either a home-study prep course or a course at a license prep school.

Home-Study Prep Courses. A home-study prep course generally requires the same background and abilities that are needed when studying the references. Additionally, although a home study course can create the study program for you, you will still have to schedule your own study periods, and stick to the schedule.

The course might be nothing more than a study manual, a course outline, and a large number of sample questions-and-answers. Or it might include additional texts, as well as computer disks and videotapes, which will increase the cost, albeit enhancing learning.

Sample questions-and-answers quickly help you find your weaknesses, while reinforcing learning points and getting you used to the mechanics of the exam. However, be careful of a tendency to memorize, questions. With the addition or deletion of just one word, two similar-looking questions might need completely different answers.

Do some questions really vary by just a word or two? Definitely. The Coast Guard keeps a database covering each subject in the exam. To prepare a specific test, they randomly select a percentage of questions from each of those subjects. Thus, today's question might read one way, while tomorrow's might read entirely the opposite. This makes it important to learn—even memorize—prin-ciples, and the way they are presented in questions, but not the questions themselves.

For many years, home-study questions (and classroom practice test questions) were keyed to exam questions but were not necessarily word-for-word copies. In August 1988, in response to a Freedom of Information Act request by Richard Block of Marine Education Textbooks, Houma, Louisiana, the Coast Guard released its 18,000-question database in both computer tape and printed form. At least one prep school organization now incorporates actual Coast Guard questions into its home-study books and software programs.[12]

License Prep Schools. Home study is not for everyone. Many a charter-boat captain will swear that he could never have obtained his license without first attending a license prep school.

The trade-off for classroom instruction is cost. This is generally the most expensive method of preparing for the exam.

A prep school can do just about everything except take the exam for you. It creates the study program; it can schedule your time to study and make you stick to the schedule; and it might even guarantee your money back if you don't pass the exam.

The instructor will teach the principles, go over sample questions, and use practice tests. He can clarify points that might be indecipherable at home. He can also help with applications and qualification forms, and steer you past bureaucratic roadblocks that sometimes tend to obscure the destination—taking and passing the exam.

Courses generally last from seven to ten days or evenings. Some schools offer weekend courses for applicants who have enough background to assimilate the material in two days. And some schools tailor their programs to the students' schedules.

For example, Houston Marine Training Services, headquartered in Kenner, Louisiana, offers a combination home-and-classroom study program called PassPak, whereby the student uses computer-assisted techniques at home and visits the local training center only when seeking specific assistance.

Some prep school organizations do not provide all the services described, or at most merely give them lip service. Shop around—and talk to the captains who know. If you select this third method of preparation, invest your money where you will get the service you need.

Which Method? Which method of preparation is best for you? Make a careful appraisal of what you know and *don't* know. Assess your chances of success with each method. Talk to a captain who had your level of knowledge when he took the exam. How many times did he have to take it to pass? Which method does he recommend? Decide how much time and money you are willing to spend in preparation. Then make your selection.

Arranging to Take the Exam

If you take a license prep course, the instructor can tell you where and when the exams are given in your area. Otherwise, contact the nearest REC (see Appendix K). One REC might interpret portions of the Coast Guard regulations differently than another. So if you have an unusual situation, and need a second opinion, you might try another REC. Bear in mind that you are prohibited from formally applying at more than one REC at the same time.

If you are living overseas, you may be able to take the exam without returning to the United States. Contact U.S. Coast Guard Headquarters, 2100 2nd Street SW, Washington, D.C. 20593, to find out which office handles your country of residence.

Limited Licenses

The Coast Guard allows special treatment in some situations. Here's an example. Under the regulations, a fishing or hunting guide who uses a boat on navigable waters in his work needs a license. Let's say that he operates a bass boat on an inland lake near his home. Must he know everything a skipper should know who takes a six-pack boat up and down the eastern seaboard for sportfishing? No.

For instance, the Coast Guard allows fishing guides on Florida's Lake Okeechobee and other freshwater lakes to operate with limited licenses. The license requirements are modified accordingly. If you are considering being a fishing or hunting guide, perhaps you can also qualify for a limited license.

Even the Boy Scouts of America benefit from limited licenses. Applicants for limited master (NC/GL/IN) licenses with four months of operating experience, and applicants for limited OUPV (six-pack) licenses (NC/GL/IN) with three months, are eligible for a limited examination if they have satisfactorily completed a boating course approved by the National Association of State Boating Law Administrators; or a public education course conducted by the U.S. Power Squadron or the American Red Cross; or a Coast Guard–approved course. The licenses are restricted to vessels being operated for the Sea Explorer program, with limitations as to size and route. They sometimes are also restricted to specific boats.

What if a nonprofit yacht club sponsors a boating class and collects fees for expenses from the students? Would a member taking a student on a boat need a license? A prudent solution to such a situation would be to send a letter to the nearest Coast Guard marine safety office, outlining the club's procedures. If the Coast Guard declares the club's school to be not-for-profit and only for pleasure, no licenses are required.

If the Coast Guard finds differently, the yacht club members involved can apply for limited licenses, as explained for the Boy Scouts. The same regulation applies to other organizations, such as established camps, educational institutions, and marinas.[13]

On the other side of the taffrail are vessels requiring special qualifications for their operators. For example, the certificate of inspection for the passenger-carrying submarine *Atlantis III* requires special license endorsements for submarine operators. A skipper authorized to operate an inspected small passenger vessel (T-boat) of at least twenty-five gross tons could qualify if he obtained an endorsement for that specific submarine.[14] To get the endorsement, he had to:

1. Complete a training program approved by the Coast Guard;

2. Have additional experience within manned submarines;

3. Have experience in the specific submarine at the site where she would be used; and

4. Pass a written examination on the safety features of the specific submarine, as well as submarines in general.

Renewals[15]

All licenses expire at the end of five years. Unlike most state driver's license agencies, the Coast Guard does not send notices of license expirations. However, it does allow for leeway. First, you can renew up to twelve months in advance. And, should you forget, you can renew up to twelve months after the license has expired. Be careful of the latter; you can't legally operate with the license during the grace period. Even if more than twelve months have passed since the expiration date, mitigating circumstances may save the day. Check with the OCMI.

Requirements for Renewal of Any License

• Either present evidence of at least one year of sea service (or acceptable substitute) during the past five years; *or*

• Pass a comprehensive open-book exercise; *or*

• Complete an approved refresher training course; *or*

• Present evidence of closely related employment for three of the previous five years, and demonstrate knowledge on an applicable Rules of the Road exercise; *and*

• Obtain a medical certification from a licensed physician or physician's assistant, including a report of visual acuity and hearing. For renewals, if an applicant has lost the sight of one eye, this does *not* disqualify, if the vision of the remaining eye is 20/400 uncorrected and 20/40 corrected.

• *Or*—you can renew "for continuity purposes," pending attainment of the renewal qualifications just described. This will prevent you from having to take either an approved course or a complete examination for subsequent renewal. However, your license will be endorsed prohibiting its use until you satisfy the renewal qualifications.

How to Renew

Either go to the the nearest REC (see Appendix K) or—now hear this!—renew by mail. Send the following material to the REC that issued the license:

1. Application on a Coast Guard–furnished form;
2. The license to be renewed, or a photocopy if it is unexpired;
3. The medical certification previously described;
4. Evidence of the required sea service, or an acceptable substitute; or the refresher training; or the closely related employment.

In the absence of sea service or any of the alternatives, the open-book exercise may be administered through the mail.

Summary

1. Anybody who carries a passenger for hire or takes passengers not for pleasure needs a license from the Coast Guard. The type of license depends upon whether the boat is inspected or uninspected, in what waters the boat will operate, and the boat's gross tonnage.

2. The hierarchy. A six-pack operator can command an uninspected vessel to one hundred gross tons. A mate (25-200 tons, GL/IN) can work under a master (GL/IN) on an inspected vessel. A mate (25-200 tons, NC) can command a six-pack (NC/IN), or work under a master (NC/IN) on an inspected vessel within his tonnage limitation. A master (25-100 GT) or an ocean/inland operator can command an inspected vessel within his tonnage limitation, and can command

a six-pack. Near-coastal licenses are valid for inland and near-coastal waters, but Great Lakes and inland licenses are not good for near-coastal waters. Ninety days of service on the Great Lakes qualifies the holder of an inland license for a Great Lakes endorsement.

3. Only U.S. citizens can qualify for licenses for inspected vessels. Non-citizens can qualify only for six-pack licenses for *undocumented* boats.

4. A sail or auxiliary sail endorsement generally requires qualifying time on the respective vessel equal to half the qualifying time needed for the license itself.

5. A progression can be followed from six-pack to mate (25-200 tons) to master (25-200 tons); or from six-pack to master (25-100/25-200 tons); or from mate (25-200 tons) to master (25-200 tons). It is also possible to qualify for a direct license as master (100 tons).

6. Any person aboard a boat can be a nonpassenger, a passenger, or a passenger for hire. A charter operator must know the distinctions.

7. The Coast Guard license exams are tough.

CHAPTER 13

Administrative Law—He Who Giveth Can Taketh Away

THE Coast Guard can make an administrative determination[1] to issue a license, document, or certificate, and it can also make an administrative decision to suspend or revoke what it has issued.

During investigations and hearings for revocation and suspension, the actions are taken against the *instrument*, not the individual. An *administrative law judge* takes action against operator licenses, and an officer in charge, marine inspection (OCMI), takes action against certificates of documentation, and certificates of inspection. The emphasis in this chapter will be upon action against operator licenses.

Coast Guard Captain Thomas W. Boerger, an OCMI, explains the system:

> We are obligated to maintain a minimum level of professional competence after licensing. This follow-up procedure is a continuing program which we carry out by investigating and holding hearing procedures for those who do not indicate minimum competence. Our purpose is remedial, not punitive, and that is why the procedures are different from what might occur in civil or criminal court.

This philosophy somewhat refutes allegations that the system grants licensing to charter captains whose only claim to competence is that they passed a classroom exam. The fact is that anybody holding a license is effectively on permanent probation, and is constantly under the spotlight.

When Does the Coast Guard Decide to Investigate?

1. If a casualty occurs due to an accident or collision;

2. If another charter operator reports an apparent violation of the regulations;

3. If a passenger, crew member, or other witness reports an apparent violation of regulations;

4. If the Coast Guard or other agency gains evidence during a boarding that appears to warrant action against the license; or

5. If by any other means the Coast Guard has reasonable grounds to suspect a violation.

The Investigation—General

An investigation does not automatically mean that the operator's boat will be seized and held for an *in rem* proceeding (action against "the thing," meaning the vessel). If the issue is simply over the captain's right to hold the license, the result could be an administrative law hearing. However, the Coast Guard can also initiate a civil penalty against any operator—whether or not he is licensed—and can proceed *in rem* to ensure the penalty will be paid.

The first job of the investigating officer (IO) is to find out what happened, in order to prevent it from happening again. So when a casualty occurs, he might come on the scene like a friendly old bloodhound, trying to help. But the instant that old bloodhound gets a whiff of a possible charge, he's going to turn into an attack dog.

So there's the dilemma. All hands involved in an incident are required by law to help the IO determine the cause.[2] Yet, if possible wrongdoing surfaces, that same IO begins a second investigation, against the license. Part 5 of 46 CFR states that no admission a person makes during an investigation may be used against him during a subsequent administrative hearing, except to prove impeachment. But the IO still *knows* what evidence he has uncovered. If he believes the licensee is guilty of something, he wants to prove it, and he has full authority to seek action against the license holder.

Does the IO's dual mission turn investigations into witch-hunts? Not necessarily. Captain Boerger says, "The Coast Guard assigns senior, experienced officers as OCMIs, and expects them to require their IOs to take balanced approaches."

Does being cooperative help? Captain Ron Wahl, founder of a national license prep school, who often receives requests for advice from his alumni, says, "I've seen too many cases of captains whose cooperation did not net them the least bit of leniency. So it's difficult for me to tell someone to be totally open with the Coast Guard in every hearing or inquiry."

So what does a captain do when an IO starts asking questions? If there's any chance that he might face charges against his license, or more, he'd better tread carefully. Although the Coast Guard at that stage is not required to read any rights against self-incrimination, a skipper should be quick to say that he would prefer to talk to his attorney before making any statement.

What Can the Investigating Officer Do?

In addition to having the power of subpoena, the IO may do any[3] of the following:

• Prefer charges. This sets the stage for a revocation and suspension hearing before an administrative law judge.

• Accept voluntary surrender of the license. In this case, the skipper permanently relinquishes all rights to the license, in exchange for not having to appear at a hearing.

• Accept voluntary deposit of the license. In case of possible mental or physical incompetence (except because of drugs), the license can be deposited with a written agreement specifying the conditions under which it will be returned. If the incompetence derives from drugs, the license can only be voluntarily surrendered.

• Refer the case to others for further action. It can go to the commandant, or to any OCMI located near the person under investigation or the witnesses.

• Give a written warning. This becomes a permanent record, but so does a record of hearing. Sometimes a charter operator will accept a written warning as an alternative that will best allow him to continue his business. If he refuses, the IO normally will prefer charges.

• Close the case.

Possible Charges.[4] Here are the possible charges that the investigating officer can prefer:

1. Misconduct, negligence, or incompetence, when acting under authority of the license. Misconduct is violation of a rule or regulation. A six-pack operator (see chapter on captain's licenses) who takes seven passengers for hire is violating a regulation in the Code of Federal Regulations. He is guilty of misconduct. Negligence stems from an act that a reasonable and prudent person of the same station, under the same circumstances, would not commit. It can also be a failure to perform in a situation where the other person would. Charges

of negligence can be subjective, based upon what the *Coast Guard* believes another captain would or would not have done. Incompetence is the inability to perform required duties. It can be due to professional deficiencies, physical disability, mental incapacity, or any combination of these. A skipper who cannot operate an onboard radar can be found guilty of incompetence. So can a captain who is under the influence of alcohol.

2. Violation of laws or regulations that apply when acting under authority of the license. A charge here can be much more serious than a misconduct charge, because it leaves the skipper wide open to criminal charges by a U.S. attorney. The law referred to is Title 46 of the U.S. Code, Subtitle II, which covers shipping, as well as "any other law or regulation intended to promote marine safety or protect navigable waters." "Acting under authority of the license" refers to being employed in the service of a vessel when either the law or the employer requires a license. It applies on board and ashore. Don't let this term sneak up and bite you. Let's say the Coast Guard doesn't require a license for a charter operation, but the employer does. As far as the Coast Guard is concerned, it's the same as if *they* required it, so all rules and regulations apply. A captain is also acting under authority of the license any time he is engaged in official matters concerning his license. This includes such actions as taking exams for endorsements or renewals, and applying for replacement licenses.

3. Conviction for a dangerous drug law violation, use of a dangerous drug, or addiction to the use of dangerous drugs. (This charge is not contingent upon the operator's acting under authority of the license.)

Specifications

The IO must prepare one or more specifications for any charge preferred. A specification is the act that the investigating officer believes you committed that, if proven, will find you guilty of the charge. There can be more than one specification pertaining to any charge.

The Administrative Law Judge

The judge is hired to conduct hearings as an administrative law judge,[5] not to try civil or criminal cases. He is a civilian, qualified to work for the Coast Guard under 5 U.S.C. 556(b). He works for the commandant, under staff supervision of the chief administrative law judge in Washington.

The administrative law judge is not something the Coast Guard invented. There are some eight hundred of these judges who are competitive career civil servants. The Coast Guard employs about ten of them.

The Office of Personnel Management (formerly Civil Service Commission) selects an administrative law judge from a register created by examinations. (Yes, even administrative law judges must sit for exams in order to get their Coast Guard tickets.) To be eligible for the exam, a candidate must have seven years of practice—in law, administrative law, or the equivalent. If he is successful with the written exam, he must pass a personal interview with other administrative law judges. Then he is eligible to sit on a Coast Guard bench.

The judge's job under the law is to help the commandant maintain minimum professional competence of license holders. To accomplish this task, the judge has the authority to admonish; suspend with or without probation; or revoke a license, document, or certificate.

Prehearing Conference

If both sides agree, the judge may hold a prehearing conference[6] to settle or simplify the issues. By this stage, the charter operator ought to have a good idea of whether the IO wants revocation, suspension, or admonishment; or whether he simply thinks the judge ought to hear the case. The operator also might gain insight into how the judge views the case. By the time a prehearing conference takes place, both sides have a reasonable idea of what might and might not be proved. Plea bargaining can be in order.

The hand of cards held by the skipper at a prehearing conference has to be played carefully. If he has an ace-in-the-hole admission or statement, he has to decide whether to play it then or to hold it. If he plays it at the conference, it can't be admitted in evidence at the later hearing, BUT the other two players—judge and IO—will know his hand when he enters the hearing.

The Hearing—General

As the representative of the Coast Guard, the IO has the burden of proof. The judge is not required to adhere strictly to the rules of evidence, although he uses the Federal Rules of Evidence as a guide. If the skipper has no professional counsel, the judge is required to let him have more latitude in presenting his case than he would a counsel. And remember: If the skipper doesn't show up, the hearing takes place without him.

Pleas

At the administrative hearing, the skipper can plead guilty, not guilty, or no contest. A guilty plea means, "I did it." A not-guilty plea means, "I'm not saying whether or not I did it. If you think I did, prove it." A no-contest plea means, "I'm not saying whether or not I did it, but I'll let you say I did it."

No-contest pleas are often used in plea bargaining, wherein the skipper tells the investigating officer (after consultation with his attorney), "You guys might spend a lot of time and money and never prove this. I'll plead no contest in exchange for . . ." What does the IO do in return? He is likely to say, "Very well, plead guilty to this one and . . ." And so it goes.

Findings

If a charge is "not proved," the judge will enter an order dismissing it. If it is found "proved," the judge will enter an order specifying whether the license is:

1. Revoked;
2. Suspended outright for a specified period after surrender;
3. Suspended for a specified period, but placed on probation for a specific period; or
4. Suspended outright for a specified period, followed by a specified period of suspension on probation.

(For guidelines for orders used by administrative law judges, see Appendix J.)

When Will the Investigating Officer Urge Revocation?[7]

The IO wants the license revoked from anyone who he believes has committed one of the following acts or offenses:

1. Assault with a dangerous weapon;
2. Misconduct resulting in loss of life or serious injury;
3. Rape or sexual molestation;
4. Murder or attempted murder;
5. Mutiny;
6. Perversion;
7. Sabotage;
8. Smuggling of aliens;
9. Incompetence;
10. Interference with the master, ship's officers, or government officials in their performance of official duties;

11. Wrongful destruction of ship's property;

12. An act or prior record indicating that continuation of the license would be a threat to the safety of life or property, or detrimental to good discipline.

When Is Revocation Mandatory?

If the judge finds a charge of *misconduct* has been proved because of wrongful possession, use, sale, or association with dangerous drugs, he *must* order the license revoked.[8] The only exception he can make concerns marijuana, if the license holder has convinced the judge that (1) he had been merely experimenting, and (2) he is "cured," and will not repeat the offense.

If the judge finds that a license holder has been convicted for violation of a dangerous drug law, use of a dangerous drug, or addiction to the use of dangerous drugs, he *must* revoke the license. Note the difference here. If the charge is *misconduct*, and the substance is marijuana, the judge has a choice. If the charge is *conviction*, he has no choice.

After the Finding

If a skipper gets an adverse finding, he has five possible avenues remaining:

1. Modification of the judge's order. If the proceeding is based upon a conviction for a dangerous drug law violation, and the respondent submits a specific court order to the effect that the conviction has been unconditionally set aside, he can request that the judge rescind the order.

2. Petition to reopen hearing. The respondent can petition on the basis of newly discovered evidence, *or* on the basis that he had been unable to appear at the hearing through no fault of his own and due to circumstances beyond his control.

3. Appeal to the commandant. Within thirty days of the judge's written decision, he can appeal to the Coast Guard commandant, who will consider only the following matters:

• Rulings on motions or objections that were not waived during the proceedings; or
• Clear errors in the record; or
• Jurisdictional questions.

If the offense was not one of those requiring mandatory revocation, or for which the IO seeks revocation (see previous section), the respondent might get a temporary license, pending results of the appeal.

4. Appeal to the National Transportation Safety Board. In cases of suspension or revocation, if the commandant's decision on appeal remains adverse, the respondent can appeal to the National Transportation Safety Board (NTSB) within ten days. If the offense was not one of those that would prohibit issuing a temporary license, the commandant may issue a stay. This could allow another temporary license until the NTSB completes its review.

5. Go to the circuit court of appeals. If the respondent feels he has a strong case, and if he has time (and money for legal fees), he should consider going to the federal court system.[9]

The World Doesn't Necessarily End Here

As soon as a year later, a person whose license was revoked or surrendered because of one or more minor offenses may apply for a new license.[10] If the license was lost because of a major offense, he might have to wait three years. However, he has the option to try any time after one year. The commandant's ultimate decision depends upon:

- Letters and recommendations from employers;
- Any other information that might influence him to approve a new license;
- The recommendation of the OCMI through whom the respondent forwards the application. (The OCMI is normally the IO's immediate boss.)

Of course, losing a license is serious business to a charter operator who depends upon it for his income. But it doesn't always mean the business has to shut down. If you have a small, family-run operation, you might see to it that your spouse gets qualifying time and a license. The same goes for children who are eighteen or older. Another option is to turn the business into a bareboat operation.

And consider the case in which loss of a license opened up a new horizon for a dive-boat operator. He had been taking divers out while his wife ran the dive shop. When his license was suspended, he bought two more boats, hired three captains, and moved ashore to run a greatly expanded dive-certification and open-water program. He even joined his students on their dives, letting his hired captain stay aboard the boat, as he was required to do.

Summary

1. The Coast Guard maintains minimum proficiency of its licensed charter captains by administrative law investigations and hearings, with the overall goal of promoting marine safety.

2. Possible charges against a license, document, or certificate are misconduct, negligence, incompetence, violation of laws and regulations, and conviction for violating dangerous drug laws.

3. An investigation and administrative law hearing can result in voluntary surrender of a license, voluntary deposit of a license, dismissal of charges, admonition, suspension, or revocation.

4. Appeals from adverse findings of an administrative law judge follow a designated chain, up to and including the federal court system.

CHAPTER 14

Bareboat Chartering for Pleasure

THE term "bareboat demise charter" has nothing to do with whether a boat is chartered with bare cupboards, or to people wearing scanty attire. As used in this chapter, a bareboat demise charter refers to placing a boat in charter for pleasure purposes in such a way that there are no passengers for hire.

First, try a multiple-choice question. Bareboating:

a. Is a way to circumvent the laws on inspected vessels.
b. Does not become legal by signing a contract.
c. Can be unsafe for owner, charter party, and captain.
d. Can be a profitable, legal way to run a chartering business.
e. Is a method of buying a boat.
f. Only (a) and (d) above.
g. (a) through (e).

Answer (g) is correct. If you disagree, wait until you finish this chapter, then reconsider. While reading the chapter, refer occasionally to Appendix B, the Coast Guard's guidelines for determining whether they believe a charter is a true bareboat demise charter.[1]

The Beginning

If skippers who take out passengers for hire must be licensed by the Coast Guard, and boats that carry more than six paying passengers must be inspected for safety, how can a bareboat charter slip through all these special rules?

It began in World War II. Because the federal government needed merchant vessel tonnage, it began acquiring and operating privately owned ships. Rather than condemn and pay for these ships, the government frequently executed demise charters with the owners.

The demise contract transferred complete possession, command, and control (navigation) of the vessel to the government, which under admiralty law was said to "stand in the shoes" of the legal owner. In real-world terms, the government became the true owner for a while—with all the privileges and responsibilities inherent in ownership. The government decided where to take the vessel, and under what conditions; then it either insured it or otherwise assumed responsibility for its replacement in case of loss. The general impression was that such a form of chartering—which worked well—was somehow limited to inspected cargo vessels.

Then came the Small Passenger Vessel Inspection Act of May 10, 1956—in the wake of several marine casualties involving loss of life on uninspected vessels that were carrying passengers for hire. Three of the more tragic incidents were the sinkings of the motor vessels *Jack* and *Pelican*, off Long Island, in separate incidents in 1951, and the loss of the sailing vessel *Levin J. Marvel* in the Chesapeake Bay in 1955. The act (now codified in Title 46, U.S.C.) reflected the will of Congress to provide protection to private citizens who go aboard small vessels as paying passengers.

At the time the act was passed, most private firms seldom used bareboat charters for pleasure. The idea of telling a customer, "My boat is now your boat. You have total responsibility, irrespective of operating conditions, and regardless of how I would prefer that you operate," was before its time. Instead, the owner often used other types of charter agreements that seemed less risky to owner and charter party alike.

Because the 1956 act identified only vessels carrying passengers or cargo for hire, it gave no consideration to demise charters of pleasure boats. So bareboat charters for pleasure were neither authorized nor denied.

What Makes It Legal?

The legality of the demise charter for pleasure derives from case law, wherein a judge's decision in one case becomes grounds for a similar decision in an ensuing case. If not overturned, such decisions build up in layers, like fiberglass on a mold, until they become as solid as statute law.

For simplicity, let's compress a group of decisions concerning bareboat charters like this: A bareboat charter that is legal by today's standards is questioned in court. After researching the 1956 act, and previously upheld decisions concerning the legality of chartered World War II cargo vessels, the judge says, "I find nothing illegal here." Subsequently, any charter operator who executes bareboat charters exactly like the one that was questioned in court is within the law.

Thus, any pleasure boat with the safety equipment required by the Coast Guard for its size and type—whether state-numbered or documented for pleasure—is a candidate for bareboating. The Coast Guard says:

> . . . It is doubtful that the Congress intended to create a specific exemption from inspection for private yachts being bareboat-chartered to carry large parties of passengers on pleasure cruises. This practice has, however, become fairly common in recent years, and has withstood most legal challenges when all of the requirements of a valid bareboat charter are complied with. Such a charter, although it may expose the charterer to considerably higher risk than the charterer would assume as a passenger aboard an inspected vessel, is a legitimate option the charterer has the freedom to choose.[2]

How Does It Work?

Let's compare three situations. First, Captain Armstrong buys a boat and documents it for pleasure. Generally, he may take out as many guests and crew members as he has personal flotation devices, because he's the owner, and he is receiving *no* direct or indirect remuneration from any passengers. He is simply having fun with his boat.

Second, he might sell that boat to Joe American, who may also take out guests and crew members. Joe will then be having fun with *his* boat.

And third, Captain Armstrong may also charter the boat to Joe. If the charter clearly makes Joe the same as the owner—and Joe takes over as any owner would—he can carry guests and crew members. He'll be having fun with his boat.

In short, if Joe obtains a true bareboat charter, he just bought the boat—for a while. As a bareboat charter operator, remind yourself once in a while that you are in effect "selling" your boat. And by selling your boat, you have circumvented the laws on inspected vessels because those laws do not apply.

An Example: A Group

A fifteen-member church group contracts with an owner to assume possession, command, and control (let's call it PCC) of a 61-foot Hatteras for a period of time. The boat is uninspected and has a state number. The group has formed the first part of a bareboat demise charter.

However, as indicated in the beginning of this chapter, a charter does not become legal merely with a contract. The contract releasing PCC to the charter group merely shows intent. Actually carrying out that intent completes the second half of a bareboat charter. The owner must in fact transfer PCC, and every member of the church group must understand that the *group* has taken over PCC. In case of routine boarding, or collision, the group must satisfy the Coast Guard that it—and not the owner or the owner's representative—was actually in charge, that it actually bought the boat.

The Ownership Clearly Must Pass to the Charter Party

Not long ago, the Coast Guard boarded a vessel with a charter group aboard. While the hired captain was returning the boat to the pier, the boarding officer questioned the members separately to determine whether he believed they had PCC. When the boat docked, the boarding officer was still undecided, until the owner came storming aboard. The boarding officer asked, "Who are you?" The owner answered, "What do you think you're doing on my boat? I'm in charge here." The Coast Guard believed he was, and declared that he had no bareboat charter.

But it's not always such a black-and-white matter. Suppose a charter party asks the owner for somebody to assist on a cruise. That might sound simple, but if the owner provides a list of possible operators, there should be enough names of available people clearly to exempt him from suspicion of collusion.

Here's an example. A bareboat charter owner/operator with an uninspected Morgan 41, documented for pleasure, contracted it to a couple new to the area. The couple asked where to find a licensed captain to help with the sailing. The operator said, "Try the guy who runs the bait shop across the pier. His son has a Coast Guard license. Maybe he's available." He was, and the Coast Guard later investigated the owner *and* the captain for operating a commercial charter business with a boat documented for pleasure.

Had the Coast Guard's case been strong enough, the incident could have cost the captain his license and the owner his boat. Farfetched? No. If the Coast Guard could have proved collusion, and could have shown that the captain had acted as the owner's agent, there would have been no bareboat charter. The boat wouldn't have been "sold."

The captain's behavior aboard the boat helped save the bareboat charter. He never acted as the owner's agent. Here is what he *didn't* do: He *didn't* say, as an extreme example, "I won't anchor over there because the owner won't allow it."

He also *didn't* say, "It's five o'clock. We're going to anchor at my favorite cove for the night, and tomorrow morning at nine o'clock, we're going over here . . ." Either statement would have indicated that he was taking over PCC.

Furthermore, the charterers behaved like owners. They brought the captain aboard to help, but retained PCC. They occasionally asked him for his interpretations of the Rules of the Road, and they asked him to notify them of shoals and other areas the boat couldn't transit safely. They gave him the helm, along with their navigational instructions. They even had him show them how to use the engine. However, as owners, they reserved final decisions to themselves.

Can the Chartering Party Hire the Boat's Regular Captain?

Sure. But the owner should take steps to show clearly that he has passed PCC and that he has made the captain and charter party understand that they are to operate within the new relationship. The Coast Guard's *Marine Safety Manual,* which is its official operating guide for carrying out the Code of Federal Regulations, says that the following provisions are indicative of a passage of PCC:

> 1. Although the master and crew are furnished by the owner, full control, possession, and navigation must be vested in the charterer.
> 2. The master and crew are paid by the charterer. [The term *charterer* means the person or persons chartering the boat from the owner.][3]

Can the Owner Himself Stay Aboard?

If the owner comes aboard as a consultant, or simply as a guest, it can be more difficult to prove that PCC was passed. In such cases, the owner should be guided by his attorney's advice. The *Marine Safety Manual* warns:

> The owner must give up his or her vessel "pro hac vice" (for the occasion) as a complete demise, turning over the incidents of ownership to the charterer: this means *complete* management, control, and operation.[4]

Are Members of the Charter Party Passengers For Hire?

If they are, then there is no bareboat charter, because the essence of bareboat chartering of a pleasure boat is that the temporary owners must *use* it for pleasure purposes. Although contracts cover this point, the charter party must understand what constitutes a passenger for hire.

Let's take an extreme example. A customer comes in, signs a demise contract on your vessel, and leaves a deposit. The following morning, eleven people arrive, one and two at a time, with checks in hand, and he shows them aboard. He then approaches you with the remainder of the charter fee, which includes his endorsements on the checks he just collected. Obviously, these guys are passengers for hire, and you stand a good chance of having your boat seized.

At the other extreme, let's look again at that church group mentioned earlier. Each member agrees to share responsibility for chartering a boat, as if he were the sole charterer. Each member contributes to a vacation charter fund during the year. The group selects one of its members to arrange the contract, and approves payment from the "First Sailing Church's Vacation Charter Fund" bank account. You probably don't have a passenger-for-hire problem.

Even if the owner and the charter party start out with a true bareboat charter, what happens if the charter group picks up a paying passenger during an overnight stopover at a marina? The Coast Guard says:

> . . . Any payment of consideration by the guests of the charterer, either to the charterer or the owner, would result in the guests being considered passengers for the purpose of the inspection statutes.[5]

The point is that for a bareboat charter to be a duck-soup operation, it must look like a duck, walk like a duck, and quack like a duck. Otherwise it's a hybrid, which makes both the temporary and the permanent owners subject to investigation.

An investigation subjects the boat to the possibility of being seized and held for action *in rem*, rather like an accused person being held without bail. In other words, it's been confiscated until the case is resolved. That could mean *months*.

But what if the charter is as legal as a Supreme Court decision? The Jones Act still must be considered.[6] Under the Jones Act, an owner or temporary owner must provide a safe working facility for crew members. Hence, if the charter party, as temporary owner, hires a captain or other crew member, it assumes the risk of suit for negligence or unseaworthiness in case its hired employee suffers injury or death.

Is It Worth the Risk?

Coast Guard Captain Thomas W. Boerger, commanding officer of a marine safety office and captain of the Port of Tampa, says flatly, "I wouldn't bareboat-charter a boat." He is speaking with the just-discussed pitfalls in mind.

Bill Chambers, president of Windward Sea Yacht Charters in Kaneohe, Hawaii, says, "Sailing conditions in Hawaii require a highly qualified and knowledgeable skipper. Bareboating is not safe." He does not intend to pass PCC, so he runs a commercial charter operation with paid captains.

But operators in many parts of the world rely heavily upon bareboat demise chartering. It is hard to argue with honest-dollar profits, and bareboat chartering brings in millions of those.

If you are thinking of executing bareboat demise charters, don't even consider starting until you have talked to one of your best friends in the charter business—your maritime attorney. And be *sure* he or she is a specialist in demise chartering and maritime affairs.

Significantly, of the nearly three hundred charter operators queried for this book, few provided sample bareboat contract forms. One respondent said that he had paid his attorney huge fees to tailor contracts for his specific operation, and he was not about to give away such proprietary information. Heed well.

Summary

1. The laws for inspected vessels do not apply to valid bareboat demise charters used only for pleasure purposes.

2. A bareboat demise contract shows only intent. To be a valid demise charter, the owner must pass possession, command, and control of the boat to the chartering party, who must exercise PCC.

3. If a bareboat chartering party takes passengers or cargo for hire on a boat that is not flagged and certified for commercial use or engages in illegal activities, the boat, the owner, the party, and the licensed captain can all be subject to legal action.

4. In spite of potential legal difficulties, valid bareboat demise chartering for pleasure has been proven to be a legal and highly profitable business.

5. Under a true bareboat demise charter, the chartering party literally buys the boat for a period of time.

CHAPTER 15

The Captain's Responsibilities

AS mentioned earlier, the Armed Forces hold a commanding officer responsible for everything his unit does or fails to do. Period.

The same philosophy applies to a captain afloat. The captain is responsible to make every decision and carry out, or have carried out, every action. He is a god, but his godliness ends when he returns to port, because his every decision and every action are subject to review and adjudication.

Fair? Probably not, but nowhere in any seafaring publication, Coast Guard regulation, CFR chapter, or public law has it ever been written that being a captain is easy, without risk . . . or fair.

To put it in a different perspective, if being a captain were easy, almost everybody would be a captain. And those who have earned the title in the crucible of command would no longer be special men and women who carry disdain for fear on their laughing faces and respect for the sea in their souls.

Safety of Vessel and Crew

Professional Captain David W. Bethany activated the EPIRB at 2030 on a February evening, while sailing from Mexico to the United States. The CSY-37 *Misty* was taking on water while beating into an unannounced and unnamed storm. Her engine was dead and her batteries dying, and the crew couldn't get ahead of the water with the manual pump. Thirty-one-year-old Bethany, emaciated from recent bouts with malaria and typhoid, had kept down neither food nor drink since getting under way three days earlier. The mate had the helm, on a watch system best described as four on and stay on.

At 1400 the day after the EPIRB was activated, a Japanese ship hove to at the sight of *Misty*'s flares. There was no common language between the two vessels. Drawing on a reserve that only a skipper trying to save his boat can find, Bethany rose, donned his wet suit and fins, and swam through the gale-swept 15-foot seas to be hauled aboard the ship. He contacted the Coast Guard on the ship's radio and swam back to his boat. With the boat hove to, he collapsed inside the leecloths of a bunk, where he remained until a Coast Guard vessel arrived to tow the boat to safety.[1]

Tact

Fisherman and radio broadcaster Mel Berman tells of the time he and his mate took a man and woman out in his 34-foot Delta sportfisherman, *Mel-Fin 3*.The charter party spent most of the time at sea in the forward cabin making love. What is a sportfishing captain's responsibility in such a case? Mel says, "Simple! The mate and I had fun fishing."

Equanimity

A major test of any captain is his ability to maintain equanimity when a client screws up. Wilson M. Hubbard, who calls himself a "waterfront character," provides an example. On one of his charter boats, a customer once hooked and successfully fought a 126-pound tarpon alongside the boat. Before Hubbard could gaff the fish, a shark came after it. Hubbard told the client to release the reel's brake, so the tarpon could escape the shark but not the line. The plan worked, and, after the shark disappeared, the customer fought the tarpon back up to the boat.

The second time he brought the tarpon alongside, Hubbard gaffed it to pull it aboard. Suddenly another shark, a 12-foot hammerhead, hit the tarpon. The shark's 3-foot-wide head interfered with its own mouth, so he kept striking at the tarpon, while lunging higher from the water with each strike. Soon the shark's head was well above the water and rising, its eyes glaring into Hubbard's eyes just inches away.

Adrenalin working overtime, Hubbard flipped the tarpon over his head—all 126 pounds of it—and tossed it into the far side of the cockpit.

Up to this point, it sounds like nothing but a sea story. And how could the client have screwed up when he did everything right?

He didn't screw up, but his wife did. Hubbard says, "That was the most exciting forty or fifty minutes in my entire life, and I knew the customer's wife was standing there shooting the whole thing with her 16-millimeter movie camera. But I was wrong. She had been too excited to remember to push the start button!"

The Social Graces

No matter how hard you try, there will always be some amenity that you haven't thought of. Dana Williams, director of Wells Yacht

Charters in Marblehead, Massachusetts, reports, "One charterer complimented us on every facet of a week-long charter except that the boat did not have a lime press!" A socially disadvantaged yacht.

Burial at Sea

Returning to the serious side, may today's captains bury at sea? Certainly. Florida charter operator David Zalewski, who scatters ashes at sea for clients, says that in his state, the cremation company (1) files a death certificate, (2) gets a permit to cremate or bury the body, and (3) sends the state a monthly report of burials. This means that a skipper can accept and scatter ashes as a personal favor to the next of kin with no special permits or reports needed, other than a log entry.

If a skipper is to operate this service commercially, he can expect to be asked for proof that he has a local occupational license, is commercially insured, and is a Coast Guard-licensed captain.

Zalewski notes that burial of a body at sea must be done in federal waters at one hundred fathoms or more.

Marriage on the High Seas

How valid is a marriage performed by a captain at sea? Admiralty attorney James O. Davis, Jr., says that the captain's authority to perform marriages is well established in the common law of admiralty. Davis, former chairman of the Standing Committee on Admiralty, American Bar Association, warns, however, that validity can hinge upon documentation from the ship's log.

For a permanent record of the marriage, a true copy or a certified copy of the log entry should be recorded in a county clerk's office after making landfall (or in an appropriate functionary's office if abroad).

Marriage in State Waters

A civil or religious marriage might avoid possible legal difficulties in proving validity of marriages at sea. A clergyman who is a skipper can perform his own marriages in state waters. So can a notary public, if marriages by notaries are legal in the state where performed. Generally, all it takes is a marriage license (procured by the prospective bride and groom), which the clergyman or notary fills out after performing the ceremony. By all means make an appropriate log entry.

Rick Smith, owner of Pisces Divers in Miami Beach, became a notary public in order to perform marriages aboard his 48-foot dive boat. He performs the marriage on board and takes the bride, groom, and wedding party to the Bahamas for a honeymoon diving trip.

Although you can obtain a notary-public commission directly from the state, the National Captain's Institute offers to cut through the red tape with a complete notary package for use in Florida waters.[2]

If you are planning to perform marriages, contact your attorney and the appropriate local marriage-license bureau to be certain of your legal authority and responsibility.

Safety Equipment

Although a captain is required by the Coast Guard to keep certain safety equipment aboard, he should consider that equipment to be the bare minimum. For example, what does the skipper of a 30-foot boat do if he uses his only two extinguishers to suppress a fire and the fire reignites? Or what does a captain do if his vessel is dead in the water and he fires his minimum supply of flares and smoke without being seen? Or consider the following case, where the Coast Guard decided a captain needed more than the minimum:

A dive-boat operator got caught in a storm with three divers down and four other members of the dive group on board. He took the passengers to shore (nearly two miles away), notified the Coast Guard, borrowed a bigger vessel, and returned for the divers. By the time he arrived, a Coast Guard vessel had safely picked up the divers.

The dive-boat skipper eventually pled no contest to negligently hazarding the lives of the three divers by leaving them in the water and returning to shore. He also pled no contest to several misconduct charges, including charges involving expired visual distress signals, unserviceable life jackets, carrying more than six passengers without a certificate of inspection, and leaving the vessel with no licensed operator aboard earlier that day to dive with the party. *And he pled no contest to a charge of negligently failing to monitor the local weather conditions by all available means.*

The dive-boat skipper said he believed he had all the required safety equipment on board, but the investigating officer and the administrative law judge were concerned that he had no means of monitoring weather conditions by radio (see chapter on administrative law). Here is a summarized version of the investigating officer's comments during a telephone interview:

It's really important to get this across to everybody concerned. After [the dive-boat skipper] departed the dock, the National Weather Service spotted a very severe storm on radar, moving rapidly toward [the skipper's location]. NOAA Weather Radio and other stations reported the information with a detailed follow-up an hour later. Meanwhile, [the skipper] was out in his boat on a clear day, incapable of knowing what those agencies were transmitting. If he had even a $20 Radio Shack receiver, he could have heard the broadcast. With that information, a reasonable person would not have started [the] dive.[3]

As a result of all charges, the skipper received an outright suspension of his license for eighteen months. He reports that he now keeps a VHF radiotelephone on each of his dive boats, even though there is nothing in writing listing such equipment as mandatory.

The Captain and the Owner

A vessel cannot have two captains at the same time, but if the owner and a paid captain are both aboard, it can sometimes seem like it. A good operating arrangement depends upon a mix of personality and an understanding of the laws and regulations. A written list of responsibilities can help prevent personality clashes during the close living conditions on board. Examples: Will the captain be responsible for the owner's children when they are aboard? Will the owner accept a chain of command from the captain to his crew? Does the owner expect the captain or crew to serve cocktails? How much spending authority is the captain allocated?

The consensus seems to be that the owner/captain relationship should be formal, and should not be allowed to deteriorate into a "we're pals" setup. Conversely, the proper employer/employee relationship should not cause the owner to treat the captain as if he owned him.

The Ultimate Responsibility

To close this book, here's possibly the biggest responsibility any captain ever has: the responsibility to notice, respect, enjoy, see, and feel what it's like to be on one of the last frontiers of this earth—the water. Take advantage of it, while making money with your boat.

Fair winds and calm seas. See you out there!

Summary

1. A captain is responsible for the safety of the vessel, passengers, and crew.

2. To be successful, a charter boat captain must take responsibility for the happiness of the passengers.

Appendices

Acknowledgments (Complete List)

The following individuals and associations provided information or assistance that was important to the preparation of this book.

American Water Ski Association
(AWSA)
Duke Cullimore, Public Relations
P.O. Box 191
Winter Haven, FL 33882

Argo Diving Services
Jon Hardy, Owner
P.O. Box 1201
Avalon, CA 90704

Arnold, Terry
Sea School
3770 16th St. N.
St. Petersburg, FL 33704

Bay Breeze Yacht Charters
Bill Allgaier, President
12917 West Bay Shore Dr.
Traverse City, MI 49684

Boerger, Thomas W., Captain
C.O., USCG Marine Safety Office
155 Columbia Dr.
Tampa, FL 33606

Briarwood on Lake Taneycomo
Bill Sheriff, Owner/Manager
P.O. Box 506
Branson, MO 65616

BVI Bareboats
Ken Maxwell, Booking Agent
91 Cannon Road
Toronto, ON M8Y 1S2 Canada

California Maritime Academy
Captain John Denham
Director of Continuing Maritime
Education
P.O. Box 1392
Vallejo, CA 94590

Caribbean Yacht Owners Assn.
Ed Cook, Fleet Manager
P.O. Box 9997
St. Thomas, VI 00801

Catalina Channel Express
Elaine Vaughan, Director of Marketing
P.O. Box 1391
San Pedro, CA 90733

Classic Charters
Bill and Jody Morison
RR 1, Box 115
Wiscasset, ME 04578

Coastline Sailing School and Yacht
Charters
Paul W. Fenn, President
Eldridge Yard Marsh Rd.
Noank, CT 06340

CSY (BVI) Ltd.
Bob Van Ost
P.O. Box 491
Tenafly, NJ 07670

Davis, James O., Jr.
Admiralty Law
696 1st Ave. N.
St. Petersburg, FL 33701

Dolphin Landings Charter Boat Center
Captain Dan, Owner/Manager
4737 Gulf Blvd.
St. Petersburg Beach, FL 33706

Edwards, Fred C.
314 Ensley Lane
Lee's Summit, MO 64081

Eleuthera-Bahamas-Charters
John and Penny Spencer, Owners
190 Widgeon Dr.
Eastham, MA 02642

Florida Sailing Charter Club
Howard Huntsberry, Owner/
President
3650 Bayhomes Dr.
Coconut Grove, FL 33133

Freya Marine Company
Attn: Sarah Fenno
909 3rd St.
Anacortes, WA 98221

G.P.S.C. Charters
Cynthia Orr, President
600 St. Andrews Rd.
Philadelphia, PA 19118

Guyer, J. Pierce, LtCdr.
USCG Marine Safety Office
155 Columbia Dr.
Tampa, FL 33606

Hinckley Yacht Charters
Patricia Tierney
Bass Harbor Marine
Bass Harbor, ME 04653

Houston Marine Training Services
T. Brantley Houston, Jr.
1600 20th St.
Kenner, LA 70062

Hubbard's Marina
Wilson M. Hubbard
150 128th Ave. W.
Madeira Beach, FL 33708

International Sailing School Ltd.
C. Van Dien, Owner
1 Matecumbe Key Rd.
Punta Gorda, FL 33955

Intrepid Charters
#7 Harbor Mall
Bellingham, WA 98225

Jody Lexow Yacht Charters
Carolyn Cox, Yacht Charter Broker
5 Brook St., P.O. Box 1207
Darien, CT 06820

Jordan, John
Legal Assistant to the Chief Judge
USCG Headquarters
2100 2nd St. SW
Washington, D.C. 20593

Jubilee Yacht Charters
Louise S. Dailey, President
972 Boston Post Rd.
Darien, CT 06820

Kime, John W., Adm.
Office of Marine Safety
USCG Headquarters
2100 2nd St. SW
Washington, D.C. 20593

Kingsley, J.W. ("Bill")
American Airlines, Inc.
MD1106, P.O. Box 619047
DFW Airport
Dallas, TX 75261

Lathrop, Les, Dockmaster
Treasure Island Tennis & Yacht Club
400 Treasure Island Causeway
Treasure Island, FL 33706

Lynn Jachney Charters
Lynn Jachney
P.O. Box 302
Marblehead, MA 01945

Marathon Divers
Jack E. Ferguson, President
12650 Overseas Highway
Marathon, FL 33050

Mel-Fin Corporation
Mel Berman, President
3224 West Kennedy
Tampa, FL 33609

Miller's Suwannee Houseboats
William R. and Billy Miller
P.O. Box 280-FS
Suwannee, FL 32692

National Association of Scuba Diving
Schools (NASDS)
Walt Amidon
641 West Willow
Long Beach, CA 90806

National Association of Underwater
Instructors (NAUI)
Tom Hemphill
P.O. Box 14650
Montclair, CA 91763

National YMCA Center for
Underwater Activities
Oakbrook Square
6083-A Oakbrook Parkway
Norcross, GA 30092

North South Yacht Charters
5915 Airport Rd., Suite 625
Mississauga, ON L4V 1T1, Canada

Ocean Voyages Inc.
Attn: Mary Crowley
1709 Bridgeway
Sausalito, CA 94965

Pacific Quest Charters
Margot Wilson, Office Manager
1521 Foreshore Walk
Granville Island
Vancouver, BC V6H 3X3, Canada

Peterson, R. D. , Capt.
Chief, USCG Public Affairs Division
Office of Boat/Public/Consumer
Affairs
2100 2nd St. SW
Washington, D.C. 20593

Pisces Divers
Rick Smith, Owner
1290 5th St.
Miami Beach, FL 33139

Professional Association of Diving
Instructors (PADI)
C. K. Stewart, Director of Marketing
1251 East Dyer Rd., Suite 100
Santa Ana, CA 92705-5605

Sailboats South Charters
John Biles, Broker/Salesman
1900 Southeast 15th St.
Fort Lauderdale, Fl 33316

St. Petersburg Yacht Charters
Page Obenshain, Owner
500 1st Ave. SE
St. Petersburg, FL 33701

San Diego Yacht Charters
John H. Dean
1880 Harbor Island Dr.
San Diego, CA 92101

San Juan Sailing
#1 Squalicum Harbor Esplanade
Bellingham, WA 98225

Scuba Schools International
Ed Christini, Executive Director
2619 Canton Ct.
Fort Collins, CO 80525

Sea Fever
P.O. Box 39-8276
Miami Beach, Fl 33139

Sea School
Ron Wahl, Founder
3770 16th St. N.
St. Petersburg, FL 33704

Shiplore Charters
Michael P. Twombly, Owner
120 Turner St.
Beaufort, NC 28516

Siben, Terri and Jeff
P.O. Box 58M
Bayshore, NY 11706

Snyder, Barry M., P.A.
Attorney at Law
2020 NE 163rd St., Suite 300
N. Miami Beach, FL 33162

Steve Colgate's Offshore Sailing
School
Ned McMahon, Operations Manager
Dept. CW, East Schofield St.
City Island, NY 10464

Strategic Marketing
Frederick J. ("Fritz") Regner, Jr.
12445 62nd St. N., Suite 303
Largo, FL 34643
[also: 65 East State St.
Columbus, OH 43215]

Suncoast Seabird Sanctuary
Ralph T. Heath, Jr., Director
18328 Gulf Blvd.
Indian Shores, FL 33535

Sun Yacht Charters Inc.
P.O. Box 737
Camden, ME 04843

Swift Yacht Charters
Harriett M. Thorpe
38 North St.
Hingham, MA 02043

Sylvia, Linda D., P.A.
Accountant and Tax Planner
4991 71st Ave. N.
Pinellas Park, FL 33565

The Moorings—USA, Inc.
Simon P. Scott, V/P Marketing
1305 U.S. 19 S., Suite 402
Clearwater, FL 33546

Tortola Yacht Charters
Myra Klaue
5825 Sunset Dr.
S. Miami, FL 33143

Treasure Island Divers, Inc.
Ron and Libby Burch, Owners
117 108th Ave.
Treasure Island, FL 33706

Truth Aquatics Inc.
Sea Landing Breakwater
Santa Barbara, CA 93109

Unger, Lester M., President
Suncoast/Pinellas SCORE Ch. #115
3021 Countryside Blvd.
Clearwater, FL 34621

U.S. Bon Appetit
Peter Kreuziger, Co-Owner
148 Marina Plaza
Dunedin, FL 34621

Virgin Islands Power Yacht Charters
(VIP)
Frank Jordan, President
P.O. Box 6760, Suite 126
Yacht Haven Marina
St. Thomas, VI 00801

Von Protz, Paul R., LtCdr.
7th Coast Guard District (mvs)
Brickell Plaza Bldg. 909 S.E. 1st Ave.
Miami, FL 33131

Wells Yacht Charters
Dana Williams, Director
91 Front St.
Marblehead, MA 01945

Windjammer Barefoot Cruises
P.O. Box 120, Dept. DD
Miami Beach, FL 33119

Windward Sea Yacht Charters
Bill Chambers, President
P.O. Box 10
Kaneohe, HI 96744

Windward Star
John's Pass
Hubbard's Marina
150 128th Ave. W.
Madeira Beach, FL 33708

Womanship
Suzanne Pogell, President
137 Conduit St.
Annapolis, MD 21401

Yacht Charter Assn. of Florida
Nancy Anderson
1323 S.E. 17th St., Suite 670
Fort Lauderdale, FL 33316

Zalewski, David
12522 68th St. N.
Largo, FL 34643

Bareboat Demise Charter Guidelines—The Coast Guard View

The following guidelines for officers in charge of marine inspection (OCMI) were extracted from the Coast Guard's Marine Safety Manual *(COMDTINST M16000.7; 10.A.4.f). (See also author's footnote at the end of this appendix.)*

Elements of Valid Bareboat Charters

The following provisions are indicative of a valid bareboat charter. Note that a valid bareboat charter does not necessarily require that all of these elements be present. Each arrangement must be evaluated on its own standing:

1. Although a master or crew may be furnished by the owner, full possession and control must be vested in the charterer. (A provision requiring the charterer to be guided by the advice of the furnished master or crew, in regard to technical matters or navigation *is* acceptable.);

2. The master and crew are paid by the charterer;

3. All food, fuel, and stores are provided by the charterer;

4. All port charges and pilotage fees are paid by the charterer;

5. Insurance is obtained by the charterer, at least to the extent of covering liability not included in the owner's insurance. A greater indication of full control in the charterer is shown if all insurance is carried by the charterer. (Of course, the owner retains every right to protect his or her interest in the vessel.);

6. The charterer may discharge, for cause, the master or any crew member without referral to the owner; or

7. The vessel is to be surveyed upon its delivery and return.

Any provision that tends to show retention of possession and control (including basic navigation) by the owner or the owner's representative should be carefully examined to see if it contradicts the claim to have created a bareboat charter.

Author's footnote. Another important provision would stipulate that the vessel may be used only for pleasure purposes by the charterer, his family, and guests, and that the vessel shall not engage in the transportation of merchandise, or carry passengers for hire, or engage in any trade in violation of the laws of the United States.

Boundary Lines

The following was extracted from 46 CFR Part 7, of October 1, 1985.

7.5 (c) Rules for establishing boundary lines. Except as otherwise described in this part, Boundary Lines are lines drawn following the general trend or the seaward, high-water shorelines and lines continuing the general trend of the seaward, high-water shorelines across entrances to small bays, inlets and rivers.

Atlantic Coast

7.10   Eastport, ME, to Cape Ann, MA.

(a) A line drawn from the easternmost extremity of Kendall Head to latitude 44°54.75′ N. longitude 66°58.5′ W.; thence to the range marker located in approximate position latitude 44°51.75′ N. longitude 66°59′ W.

(b) A line drawn from West Quoddy Head Light to latitude 44°48.5′ N. longitude 66°56.4′ W. (Sail Rock Lighted Whistle Buoy "1"); thence to latitude 44°37.5′ N. longitude 67°09.8′ W. (Little River Lighted Whistle Buoy "2LR"); thence to latitude 44°14.15′ N. longitude 67°57.2′ W. (Frenchman Bay Approach Lighted Whistle Buoy "FB"); thence to Mount Desert Light; thence to Matinicus Rock Light; thence to Monhegan Island Light; thence to latitude 43°31.6′ N. longitude 70°05.5′ W. (Portland Lighted Horn Buoy "P"); thence to Boon Island Light; thence to latitude 42°37.9′ N. longitude 70°31.2′ W. (Cape Ann Lighted Whistle Buoy "2").

7.15   Massachusetts Bay, MA.

A line drawn from latitude 42°37.9′ N. longitude 70°31.2′ W. (Cape Ann Lighted Whistle Buoy "2") to latitude 42° 22.7′ N. longitude 70°47.0′ W. (Boston Lighted Horn Buoy "B"); thence to Race Point Light.

7.20   Nantucket Sound, Vineyard Sound, Buzzards Bay, Narragansett Bay, MA, Block Island Sound and easterly entrance to Long Island Sound, NY.

(a) A line drawn from Chatham Light to latitude 41°36.1′ N. longitude 69°51.1′ W. (Pollack Rip Entrance Lighted Horn Buoy "PR"); thence to latitude 41°26.0′ N. longitude 69°46.2′ W. (Great Round Shoal Channel Lighted Buoy "2"); thence to Sankaty Head Light.

(b) A line drawn from the westernmost extremity of Nantucket Island to the southwesternmost extremity of Wasque Point, Chappaquiddick Island.

(c) A line drawn from Gay Head Light to Block Island Southeast Light; thence to Montauk Point Light on the easterly end of Long Island.

7.25   Montauk Point, NY, to Atlantic Beach, NY.

(a) A line drawn from Shinnecock East Breakwater Light to Shinnecock West Breakwater Light.

(b) A line drawn from Moriches Inlet East Breakwater Light to Moriches Inlet West Breakwater Light.

(c) A line drawn from Fire Island Inlet Breakwater Light 348 degrees true to the southernmost extremity of the spit of land at the western end of Oak Beach.

(d) A line drawn from Jones Inlet Light 322 degrees true across the southwest tangent of the island on the north side of Jones Inlet to the shoreline.

7.30   New York Harbor, NY.

A line drawn from East Rockaway Inlet Breakwater Light to Ambrose Light; thence to Highlands Light (north tower).

7.35   Sandy Hook, NJ, to Cape May, NJ.

(a) A line drawn from Shark River Inlet North Breakwater Light "2" to Shark River Inlet South Breakwater Light "1".

(b) A line drawn from Manasquan Inlet North Breakwater Light to Manasquan Inlet South Breakwater Light.

(c) A line drawn along the submerged Barnegat Inlet North Breakwater to Barnegat Inlet North Breakwater Light "2"; thence to Barnegat Inlet Light "5"; thence along the submerged Barnegat Inlet South Breakwater to shore.

(d) A line drawn from the seaward tangent of Long Beach Island to the seaward tangent of Pullen Island across Beach Haven and Little Egg Inlets.

(e) A line drawn from the seaward tangent of Pullen Island to the seaward tangent of Brigantine Island across Brigantine Inlet.

(f) A line drawn from the seaward extremity of Absecon Inlet North Jetty to Atlantic City Light.

(g) A line drawn from the southernmost point of Longport at latitude 39°18.2' N. longitude 74°32.2' W. to the northeasternmost point of Ocean City at latitude 39°17.6' N. longitude 74° 33.1' W. across Great Egg Harbor Inlet.

(h) A line drawn parallel with the general trend of the seaward, high-water shoreline across Corson Inlet.

(i) A line formed by the centerline of the Townsend Inlet Highway Bridge.

(j) A line formed by the shoreline of Seven Mile Beach and Hereford Inlet Light.

7.40   Delaware Bay and tributaries.

A line drawn from Cape May Inlet East Jetty Light to latitude 38° 55.8' N. longitude 74°51.4 W'. (Cape May Harbor Inlet Lighted Bell Buoy "2CM"); thence to latitude 38°48.9′ N. longitude 75°02.3′ W. (Delaware Bay Entrance Channel Lighted Buoy "8"); thence to the northernmost extremity of Cape Henlopen.

7.45   Cape Henlopen, DL, to Cape Charles, VA.

(a) A line drawn from the easternmost extremity of Indian River Inlet North Jetty to latitude 38°36.5′ N. longitude 75°02.8′ W. (Indian River Inlet Lighted Gong Buoy "1"); thence to Indian River Inlet South Jetty Light.

(b) A line drawn from Ocean City Inlet Light "6" to latitude 38°19.4′ N. longitude 75°05.0′ W. (Ocean City Inlet Entrance Lighted Buoy "4"); thence to latitude 38°19.3′ N. longitude 75°05.1′ W. (Ocean City Inlet Entrance Lighted Buoy "5"); thence to the easternmost extremity of the south breakwater.

(c) A line drawn from Assateague Beach Tower Light to latitude 37° 50.2′ N. longitude 75°24.9′ W. (Chincoteague Inlet Lighted Bell Buoy "CI"); thence to the tower charted at latitude 37°52.6′ N. longitude 75°26.7′ W.

(d) A line drawn from the southernmost extremity of Cedar Island to latitude 37°34.7′ N. longitude 75°36.0′ W. (Wachapreague Inlet Entrance Lighted Buoy "1"); thence due south to shore at Parramore Beach.

(e) A line drawn from the seaward tangent of Parramore Beach to the lookout tower on the northern end of Hog Island charted in approximate position latitude 37°27.2′ N. longitude 75°40.5′ W.

7.50   Chesapeake Bay and tributaries.

A line drawn from Cape Charles Light to latitude 36°56.8′ N. longitude 75°55.1′ W. (North Chesapeake Entrance Lighted Gong Buoy "NCD"); thence to latitude 36°54.8′ N. longitude 75°55.6′ W. (Chesapeake Bay Entrance Lighted Bell Buoy "CBC"); thence to latitude 36°55.0′ N. longitude 75°58.0′ W. (Cape Henry Buoy "1"); thence to Cape Henry Light.

7.55   Cape Henry, VA, to Cape Fear, NC.

(a) A line drawn from Rudee Inlet Jetty Light "2" to latitude 36°50′ N. longitude 75°56.7′ W.; thence to Rudee Inlet Jetty Light "1".

(b) A line drawn from Bodie Island Light to latitude 35°49.3′ N. longitude 75°31.9′ W. (Oregon Inlet Approach Lighted Whistle Buoy "OI"); thence to Oregon Inlet Radiobeacon.

(c) A line drawn from Hatteras Inlet Light 255 degrees true to the eastern end of Ocracoke Island.

(d) A line drawn from the westernmost extremity of Ocracoke Island at latitude 35°04′ N. longitude 76°00.8′ W. to the northeasternmost extremity of Portsmouth Island at latitude 35°03.7′ N. longitude 76°02.3′ W.

(e) A line drawn across Drum Inlet parallel with the general trend of the seaward, high-water shoreline.

(f) A line drawn from the southernmost extremity of Cape Lookout to latitude 34°38′ N. longitude 76°40.6′ W. (Beaufort Inlet Lighted Bell Buoy "2BI"); thence to the seaward extremity of the Beaufort Inlet West Jetty.

(g) A line drawn from the seaward extremity of Masonboro Inlet North Jetty to latitude 34°10.3′ N. longitude 77°48.0′ W. (Masonboro Inlet Lighted Whistle Buoy "A"); thence to the beach in approximate position latitude 34°10′ N. longitude 77°49.4′ W.

7.60   Cape Fear, NC, to Sullivans Island, SC.

(a) A line drawn from the southernmost extremity of Cape Fear to latitude 33°49.5′ N. longitude 78°03.7′ W. (Cape Fear River Entrance Lighted Bell Buoy "2CF"); thence to Oak Island Light.

(b) A line drawn from the southernmost extremity of Bird Island at approximate position latitude 33°51.2′ N. longitude 78°32.6′ W. to latitude 33°50.3′ N. longitude 78°32.5′ W. (Little River Inlet Entrance Lighted Whistle Buoy "2LR"); thence to the northeasternmost extremity of Waties Island at approximate position latitude 33°51.2′ N. longitude 78°33.6′ W.

(c) A line drawn from the seaward extremity of Murrells Inlet North Jetty to latitude 33°31.5′ N. longitude 79°01.6′ W. (Murrells Inlet Lighted Bell Buoy "MI"); thence to Murrells Inlet South Jetty Light.

(d) A line drawn from Georgetown Light to latitude 33°11.6′ N. longitude 79°05.4′ W. (Winyah Bay Lighted Bell Buoy "2WB"); thence to the southernmost extremity of Sand Island.

7.65   Charleston Harbor, SC.

A line drawn from Charleston Light on Sullivans Island to latitude 32°40.7′ N. longitude 79°42.9′ W. (Charleston Lighted Whistle Buoy "2C"); thence to Folly Island Loran Tower (latitude 32° 41.0′ N. longitude 79°53.2′ W.)

7.70   Folly Island, SC, to Hilton Head Island, SC.

(a) A line drawn from the southernmost extremity of Folly Island to latitude 32°35′ N. longitude 79°58.2′ W. (Stono Inlet Lighted Whistle Buoy "1S"); thence to Kiawah Island bearing approximately 307 degrees true.

(b) A line drawn from the southernmost extremity of Kiawah Island to latitude 32°31′ N. longitude 80°07.8′ W. (North Edisto River Entrance Lighted Whistle Buoy "2NE"); thence to Botany Bay Island in approximate position latitude 32°33.1′ N. longitude 80°12.7′ W.

(c) A line drawn from the microwave antenna tower on Edisto Beach charted in approximate position latitude 32°29.3′ N. longitude 80°19.2′ W. across St. Helena Sound to the abandoned lighthouse tower on Hunting Island charted in approximate position latitude 32°22.5′ N. longitude 80°26.5′ W.

(d) A line drawn from the abandoned lighthouse on Hunting Island in approximate position latitude 32°22.5′ N. longitude 80°26.2′ W. to latitude 32°18′ N. longitude 80°25′ W.; thence to the standpipe on Fripp Island in approximate position latitude 32°19′ N. longitude 80°28.7′ W.

(e) A line drawn from the westernmost extremity of Bull Point on Capers Island to latitude 32°04.8′ N. longitude 80°34.9′ W. (Port Royal Sound Lighted

Whistle Buoy "2PR"); thence to the easternmost extremity of Hilton Head at latitude 32°13.2′ N. longitude 80° 40.1′ W.

7.75   Savannah River/Tybee Roads.

A line drawn from the southwesternmost extremity of Braddock Point to latitude 31°58.3′ N. longitude 80°44.1′ W. (Tybee Lighted Whistle Buoy "T"); thence to the southeasternmost extremity of Little Tybee Island bearing approximately 269 degrees true.

7.80   Tybee Island, GA, to St. Simons Island, GA.

(a) A line drawn from the southernmost extremity of Savannah Beach on Tybee Island 255 degrees true across Tybee Inlet to the shore of Little Tybee Island south of the entrance to Buck Hammock Creek.

(b) A line drawn from the southernmost extremity of Little Tybee Island at Beach Hammock to the easternmost extremity of Wassaw Island.

(c) A line drawn from Wassaw Island in approximate position latitude 31°52.5′ N. longitude 80°58.5′ W. to latitude 31°48.3′ N. longitude 80°56.8′ W. (Ossabaw Sound North Channel Buoy "OS"); thence to latitude 31°39.3′ N. longitude 81°02.3′ W. (St. Catherines Sound Buoy "St. C."); thence to latitude 31°31.2′ N. longitude 81°03.8′ W. (Sapelo Sound Buoy "S"); thence to the easternmost extremity of Blackbeard Island at Northeast Point.

(d) A line drawn from the southernmost extremity of Blackbeard Island to latitude 31°19.4′ N. longitude 81°11.5′ W. (Doboy Sound Lighted Buoy "D"); thence to latitude 31°04.1′ N. longitude 81°16.7′ W. (St. Simons Lighted Whistle Buoy "ST S").

7.85   St. Simons Island, GA, to Little Talbot Island, FL.

(a) A line drawn from latitude 31°04.1′ N. longitude 81° 16.7′ W. (St. Simons Lighted Whistle Buoy "ST S") to latitude 30°42.7′ N. longitude 81°19.0′ W. (St. Mary's Entrance Lighted Whistle Buoy "1"); thence to Amelia Island Light.

(b) A line drawn from the southernmost extremity of Amelia Island to latitude 30°29.4′ N. longitude 81°22.9′ W. (Nassau Sound Approach Buoy "6A"); thence to the northeasternmost extremity of Little Talbot Island.

7.90   St. Johns River, FL.

A line drawn from the southeasternmost extremity of Little Talbot (Spike) Island to latitude 30°23.8′ N. longitude 81°20.3′ W. (St. Johns Lighted Whistle Buoy "2STJ"); thence to St. Johns Light.

7.95   St. Johns Point, FL, to Miami Beach, FL.

(a) A line drawn from the seaward extremity of St. Augustine Inlet North Jetty to latitude 29°55′ N. longitude 81°15.3′ W. (St. Augustine Lighted Whistle Buoy "ST.A."); thence to the seaward extremity of St. Augustine Inlet South Jetty.

(b) A line formed by the centerline of the highway bridge over Matanzas Inlet.

(c) A line drawn from the seaward extremity of Ponce de Leon Inlet north jetty to latitude 29°04.7′ N. longitude 80°54′ W. (Ponce de Leon Inlet Lighted Bell Buoy "2"); thence to Ponce de Leon Inlet Approach Light.

(d) A line drawn from Canaveral Harbor Approach Channel Range Front Light to latitude 28°23.7′ N. longitude 80°32.2′ W. (Canaveral Bight Wreck Lighted Buoy "WR6"); thence to the radio tower on Canaveral Peninsula in approximate position latitude 28°22.9′ N. longitude 80°36.6′ W.

(e) A line drawn across the seaward extremity of the Sebastian Inlet Jetties.

(f) A line drawn from the seaward extremity of the Fort Pierce Inlet North Jetty to latitude 27°28.5′ N. longitude 80°16.2′ W. (Fort Pierce Inlet Lighted Whistle Buoy "2"); thence to the tank located in approximate position latitude 27°27.2′ N. longitude 80°17.2′ W.

(g) A line drawn from the seaward extremity of St. Lucie Inlet North Jetty to latitude 27°10′ N. longitude 80°08.4′ W. (St. Lucie Inlet Entrance Lighted Whistle Buoy "2"); thence to Jupiter Island bearing approximately 180 degrees true.

(h) A line drawn from the seaward extremity of Jupiter Inlet North Jetty to the northeast extremity of the concrete apron on the south side of Jupiter Inlet.

(i) A line drawn from the seaward extremity of Lake Worth Inlet North Jetty to latitude 26°46.4′ N. longitude 80°01.5′ W. (Lake Worth Inlet Lighted Bell Buoy "2LW"); thence to Lake Worth Inlet Lighted Buoy "3"; thence to the seaward extremity of Lake Worth Inlet South Jetty.

(j) A line drawn across the seaward extremity of the Boynton Inlet Jetties.

(k) A line drawn from Boca Raton Inlet North Jetty Light "2" to Boca Raton Inlet South Jetty Light "1".

(l) A line drawn from Hillsboro Inlet Light to Hillsboro Inlet Entrance Light "2"; thence to Hillsboro Inlet Entrance Light "1"; thence west to the shoreline.

(m) A line drawn from the tower located in approximate position latitude 26°06.9′ N. longitude 80°06.4′ W. to latitude 26°05.5′ N. longitude 80°04.8′ W. (Port Everglades Lighted Whistle Buoy "1"); thence to the signal tower located in approximate position latitude 26°05.5′ N. longitude 80°06.5′ W.

(n) A line drawn from the seaward extremity of Bakers Haulover Inlet North Jetty 090 degrees true to longitude 80°07.2′ W.; thence to the seaward extremity of Bakers Haulover Inlet South Jetty.

7.100 Florida Reefs and Keys from Miami, FL, to Marquesas Keys, FL.

(a) A line drawn from the tower located in approximate position latitude 25°46.7′ N. longitude 80°08′ W. to latitude 25°46.1′ N. longitude 80°05′ W. (Miami Lighted Whistle Buoy "M"); thence to Fowey Rocks Light (latitude 25°35.4′ N. longitude 80° 05.8′ W.); thence to Pacific Reef Light (latitude 25°22.3′ N. longitude 80°08.5′ W.); thence to Carysfort Reef Light (latitude 25°13.3′ N. longitude 80°12.7′ W.); thence to Molasses Reef Light "10" (latitude 25°00.7′ N. longitude 80°22.6′ W.); thence to Alligator Reef Light (latitude 24°51.1′ N. longitude 80°37.1′

W.); thence to Tennessee Reef Light (latitude 24°44.7′ N. longitude 80°46.9′ W.); thence to Sombrero Key Light (latitude 24°37.6′ N. longitude 81°06.6′ W.); thence to American Shoal Light (latitude 24°31.5′ N. longitude 81°31.2′ W.); thence to latitude 24°27.7′ N. longitude 81°48.1′ W. (Key West Entrance Lighted Whistle Buoy); thence to Cosgrove Shoal Light (latitude 24°27.5′ N. longitude 82°11.2′ W.); thence due north to a point 12 miles from the baseline from which the territorial sea is measured in approximate position latitude 24°47.5′ N. longitude 82°11.2′ W.

Gulf Coast

7.105 Marquesas Keys, FL, to Rio Grande, TX.

(a) A line drawn from Marquesas Keys, Florida, at approximate position latitude 24°47.5′ N. longitude 82°11.2′ W. along the 12-mile line which marks the seaward limits of the contiguous zone (as defined in 33 CFR Part 2.05-15) to Rio Grande, Texas, at approximate position latitude 25°58.6′ N. longitude 96°55.5′ W.

Hawaii

7.110 Mamala Bay, HI.

(a) A line drawn from Barbers Point Light to Diamond Head Light.

Pacific Coast

7.115 Santa Catalina Island, CA.

(a) A line drawn from the northernmost point of Lion Head to the north tangent of Bird Rock Island; thence to the northernmost point of Blue Cavern Point.

(b) A line drawn from White Rock to the northernmost point of Abalone Point.

7.120 Mexican/United States Border to Point Fermin, CA.

(a) A line drawn from the southerly tower of the Coronado Hotel in approximate position latitude 32°40.8′ N. longitude 117°10.6′ W. to latitude 32°39.1′ N. longitude 117°13.6′ W. (San Diego Bay Channel Lighted Bell Buoy "5"); thence to Point Loma Light.

(b) A line drawn from Mission Bay South Jetty Light "2" to Mission Bay North Jetty Light "1".

(c) A line drawn from Oceanside South Jetty Light "4" to Oceanside Breakwater Light "3".

(d) A line drawn from Dana Point Jetty Light "6" to Dana Point Breakwater Light "5".

(e) A line drawn from Newport Bay East Jetty Light "4" to Newport Bay West Jetty Light "3".

(f) A line drawn from Anaheim Bay East Jetty Light "6" to Anaheim Bay West Jetty Light "5"; thence to Long Beach Breakwater East End Light "1". A line drawn from Long Beach Entrance Light "2" to Long Beach Light. A line drawn from Los Angeles Main Channel Entrance Light "2" to Los Angeles Light.

7.125 Point Vincente, CA, to Point Conception, CA.

(a) A line drawn from Redondo Beach East Jetty Light "2" to Redondo Beach West Jetty Light "3".

(b) A line drawn from Marina Del Rey Light "4" to Marina Del Rey Breakwater South Light "1". A line drawn from Marina Del Rey Breakwater North Light "2" to Marina Del Rey Light "3".

(c) A line drawn from Port Hueneme East Jetty Light "4" to Port Hueneme West Jetty Light "3".

(d) A line drawn from Channel Islands Harbor South Jetty Light "2" to Channel Islands Harbor Breakwater South Light "1". A line drawn from Channel Islands Harbor Breakwater North Light to Channel Islands Harbor North Jetty Light "5".

(e) A line drawn from Ventura Marina South Jetty Light "6" to Ventura Marina Breakwater South Light "3". A line drawn from Ventura Marina Breakwater North Light to Ventura Marina North Jetty Light "7".

(f) A line drawn from Santa Barbara Harbor Light "4" to latitude 34°24.1′ N. longitude 119°40.7′ W. (Santa Barbara Harbor Lighted Bell Buoy "1"); thence to Santa Barbara Harbor Breakwater Light.

7.130 Point Conception, CA, to Point Sur, CA.

(a) A line drawn from the southernmost extremity of Fossil Point at longitude 120°43.5′ W. to the seaward extremity of Whaler Island Breakwater.

(b) A line drawn from the outer end of Morro Bay Entrance East Breakwater to latitude 35°21.5′ N. longitude 120°52.3′ W. (Morro Bay Entrance Lighted Bell Buoy "1"); thence to Morro Bay West Breakwater Light.

7.135 Point Sur, CA, to Cape Blanco, OR.

(a) A line drawn from Monterey Harbor Light "6" to latitude 36°36.5′ N. longitude 121°53.2′ W. (Monterey Harbor Anchorage Buoy "A"); thence to the northernmost extremity of Monterey Municipal Wharf No. 2.

(b) A line drawn from the seaward extremity of the pier located 0.3 mile south of Moss Landing Harbor Entrance to the seaward extremity of the Moss Landing Harbor North Breakwater.

(c) A line drawn from Santa Cruz Light to the southernmost projection of Soquel Point.

(d) A straight line drawn from Point Bonita Light across Golden Gate through Mile Rocks Light to the shore.

(e) A line drawn from the northwestern tip of Tomales Point to latitude 38°15.1′ N. longitude 123°00.1′ W. (Tomales Point Lighted Horn Buoy "2"); thence to latitude 38°17.2′ N. longitude 123°02.3′ W. (Bodega Harbor Approach Lighted Gong Buoy "BA"); thence to the southernmost extremity of Bodega Head.

(f) A line drawn from Humboldt Bay Entrance Light "4" to Humboldt Bay Entrance Light "3".

(g) A line drawn from Crescent City Outer Breakwater Light "5" to the southeasternmost extremity of Whaler Island at longitude 124°11′ W.

7.140 Cape Blanco, OR, to Cape Flattery, WA.

(a) A line drawn from the seaward extremity of the Coos Bay South Jetty to latitude 43°21.9′ N. longitude 124°21.7′ W. (Coos Bay Entrance Lighted Bell Buoy "1"); thence to the seaward extremity of the Coos Bay North Jetty.

(b) A line drawn from the lookout tower located in approximate position latitude 46°13.6′ N. longitude 124°00.7′ W. to latitude 46°12.8′ N. longitude 124°08′ W. (Columbia River Entrance Lighted Whistle Buoy "2"); thence to latitude 46°14.5′ N. longitude 124°09.5′ W. (Columbia River Entrance Lighted Bell Buoy "1"); thence to North Head Light.

(c) A line drawn from latitude 46°52.8′ N. longitude 124°12.6′ W. (Grays Harbor Light to Grays Harbor Entrance Lighted Whistle Buoy "2"); thence to latitude 46°55′ N. longitude 124°14.7′ W. (Grays Harbor Entrance Lighted Whistle Buoy "3"); thence to Grays Harbor Bar Range Rear Light.

7.145 Strait of Juan de Fuca, Haro Strait, and Strait of Georgia, WA.

(a) A line drawn from the northernmost point of Angeles Point to latitude 48°21.1′ N. longitude 123°02.5′ W. (Hein Bank Lighted Bell Buoy); thence to latitude 48°25.5′ N. longitude 122°58.5′ W. (Salmon Bank Lighted Gong Buoy "3"); thence to Cattle Point Light on San Juan Island.

(b) A line drawn from Lime Kiln Light to Kellett Bluff Light on Henry Island; thence to Turn Point Light on Stuart Island; thence to Skipjack Island Light; thence to latitude 48°46.6′ N. longitude 122°53.4′ W. (Clements Reef Buoy "2"); thence to International Boundary Range B Front Light.

Alaska

7.150 Canadian (BC) and United States (AK) Borders to Cape Spencer, AK.

(a) A line drawn from the northeasternmost extremity of Point Mansfield, Sitklan Island 040 degrees true to the mainland.

(b) A line drawn from the southeasternmost extremity of Island Point, Sitklan Island, to the southernmost extremity of Garnet Point, Kanagunut Island; thence to Lord Rock Light; thence to Barren Island Light; thence to Cape Chacon Light; thence to Cape Muzon Light.

(c) A line drawn from Point Cornwallis Light to Cape Bartolome Light; thence to Cape Edgecumbe Light; thence to the westernmost extremity of Cape Cross.

(d) A line drawn from Surge Bay Entrance Light to Cape Spencer Light.

7.155　Cape Spencer, AK, to Cape St. Elias, AK.

(a) A line drawn from the westernmost extremity of Harbor Point to the southernmost extremity of LaChaussee Spit at Lituya Bay.

(b) A line drawn from Ocean Cape Light to latitude 59°31.9′ N. longitude 139°57.1′ W. (Yakutat Bay Entrance Lighted Whistle Buoy "2"); thence to the southeasternmost extremity of Point Manby.

(c) A line drawn from the northernmost extremity of Point Riou to the easternmost extremity of Icy Cape.

7.160　Point Whitshed, AK, to Aialik Cape, AK.

(a) A line drawn from the southernmost extremity of Point Whitshed to the easternmost extremity of Hinchinbrook Island.

(b) A line drawn from Cape Hinchinbrook Light to Schooner Rock Light "1".

(c) A line drawn from the southwesternmost extremity of Montague Island to Point Elrington Light; thence to the southernmost extremity of Cape Puget.

(d) A line drawn from the southernmost extremity of Cape Resurrection to the Aialik Cape.

7.165　Kenai Peninsula, AK, to Kodiak Island, AK.

(a) A line drawn from the southernmost extremity of Kenai Peninsula at longitude 151°44′ W. to East Amatuli Island Light; thence to the northwesternmost extremity of Shuyak Island at Party Cape; thence to the easternmost extremity of Cape Douglas.

(b) A line drawn from the southernmost extremity of Pillar Cape on Afognak Island to Spruce Cape Light; thence to the easternmost extremity of Long Island; thence to the northeasternmost extremity of Cape Chiniak.

(c) A line drawn from Cape Nunilak at latitude 58°09.7′ N. to the northernmost extremity of Raspberry Island. A line drawn from the westernmost extremity of Raspberry Cape to the northernmost extremity of Miners Point.

7.170　Alaska Peninsula, AK, to Aleutian Islands, AK.

(a) A line drawn from the southernmost extremity of Cape Kumlium to the westernmost extremity of Nakchamik Island; thence to the easternmost extremity of Castle Cape at Chignik Bay.

(b) A line drawn from Second Priest Rock to Ulakta Head Light at Iliuliuk Bay entrance.

(c) A line drawn from Arch Rock to the northernmost extremity of Devilfish Point at Captains Bay.

(d) A line drawn from the easternmost extremity of Lagoon Point to the northwesternmost extremity of Cape Kutuzof at Port Moller.

7.175　Alaska Peninsula, AK, to Nunivak, AK.

(a) A line drawn from the northernmost extremity of Goose Point at Egegik Bay to Protection Point.

(b) A line drawn from the westernmost extremity of Kulukak Point to the northernmost extremity of Round Island; thence to the southernmost extremity of Hagemeister Island; thence to the southernmost extremity of Cape Peirce; thence to the southernmost extremity of Cape Newenham.

(c) A line drawn from the church spire located in approximate position latitude 59°45′ N. longitude 161°55′ W. at the mouth of the Kanektok River to the southernmost extremity of Cape Avinof.

7.180 Kotzebue Sound, AK.

(a) A line drawn from Cape Espenberg Light to latitude 66°52′ N. longitude 163°28′ W.; and thence to Cape Krusenstern Light.

Dive Certification Agencies (Partial List)

National Association of Scuba Diving Schools (NASDS)
641 West Willow
Long Beach, CA 90806
(213) 595-5361

National YMCA Center for Underwater Activities
Oakbrook Square
6083-A Oakbrook Parkway
Norcross, GA 30092
(404) 662-5172

National Association of Underwater Instructors (NAUI)
P.O. Box 14650
Montclair, CA 91763
(714) 621-5801

Professional Association of Diving Instructors (PADI)
1251 East Dyer Road, Suite 100
Santa Ana, CA 92705-5605
(800) 722-7234

Scuba Schools International, Inc. (SSI)
2619 Canton Court
Fort Collins, CO 80525
(303) 482-0883

Documentation Requirements and Forms

For initial documentation of a new or used boat, see section I below—Requirements for First-Time Documentation. For changes to existing documentation, such as owner changes, vessel name changes, etc., see section II below—Subsequent Transactions. For the special cases (wrecked, forfeited, or captured vessels, or special legislation products), refer to section III. When buying or selling in connection with documentation, see hints in section IV.

I. Requirements for First-Time Documentation

Applies to all vessels except those classified as specially qualified (captured, forfeited, wrecked, or specially authorized by Congress to operate in coastwise trade, Great Lakes trade, or the fisheries).

Certificate	Vessel	Requirements
Registry	New	1. Application form (CG-1258)
		2. Tonnage evidence (CG-5397)
		3. Marking evidence (CG-1322)
		4. Build evidence (CG-1261)
	Used	1. Application form
		2. Tonnage evidence
		3. Marking evidence
		4. Copy of last flagging action
		5. Evidence of removal from foreign registry (if was foreign flagged)
		6. Chain of title since last flagging
		7. Citizenship declaration (MA-899)
		8. Recording fee

Coastwise, or Great Lakes	New	Same as Registry (New) 1-4
	Used	1-4. Same as Registry (New) 1-4 5. Complete chain of title 6. Citizenship evidence for all owners in chain 7. Citizenship declaration 8. Recording fee
Fishery	New	Same as Registry (New) 1-4
	Used	1-4. Same as Registry (New) 1-4 5-9. Same as Registry (Used) 4-8
Pleasure	New	1-4. Same as Registry (New) 1-4 5. Fee
	Used	1-3. Same as Registry (New) 1-3 4. Fee 5-9. Same as Registry (Used) 4-8
		OR (at owner's option)
Pleasure	Used	1-5. Same as Pleasure (New) 1-5 6-9. Same as Coastwise (Used) 5-8

II. Subsequent Transactions

Applies to all vessels covered under section I—Requirements for First-Time Documentation.

Transaction	*Requirements*
Renewal (annually)	Renewal application (CG-1280)
Surrender (for changes) *V*essel Name	1. Application form (CG-1258) 2. Certificate of documentation (CG-1270) 3. Mortgagee consent (CG-4593) 4. Marking evidence (CG-1322) 5. Fee

Home Port	1-4. Same as Vessel Name change 1-4 5. Fee (for Pleasure vessels only) 6. Abstract of title
Ownership	1-3. Same as Vessel Name change 1-3 4. Fee (for Pleasure vessels only) 5. Title evidence (Bill of Sale et al.) 6. Recording fee 7. Citizenship declaration (MA-899)
General Partner	Same as Ownership change 1-5
Tonnage/Dimensions	1-4. Same as Ownership change 1-4 5. Tonnage evidence (CG-5397)
Vessel Restrictions	Same as Ownership change 1-4
Owner Name	1-3. Same as Vessel Name change 1-3 4. Title evidence (Proof of change)
Death of Tenant by the Entirety	1-3. Same as Vessel Name change 1-3 4. Title evidence (Proof of change)
Propulsion	Same as Vessel Name change 1-2
Trade Endorsement	1-2. Same as Vessel Name change 1-2 3. Title evidence 4. Fee (for Pleasure vessels only) 5. Marking evidence
Non-U.S. Captain	1. Certificate of documentation
Return to U.S. Captain	1-2. Same as Vessel Name change 1-2 3. Statement of return 4. Fee (for Pleasure vessels only)
Document Office Error	1. Certificate of documentation
Owner Address	1. Letter

Certificate Replacement
   No Blank Spaces   1-2. Same as Vessel Name change 1-2
                                      3. Fee (for Pleasure vessels only)

   Mutilated   1-3. Same as No Blank Spaces
                                         1-3 above

   Certificate Lost   1. Application form (CG-1258)
                                      2. Fee (for Pleasure vessels only)

   Wrongfully Withheld   1. Application form (CG-1258)
                                      2. Statement

Deletion of Certificate
   Vessel sold to alien
   or flagged foreign   1. Certificate of documentation
                                      2. Consent of Maritime
                                         Administration

   Failure to renew or
   surrender   1. Automatic upon discovery
                                         or failure

Forward certificate for deletion when: Owner no longer citizen;
owner no longer elects documentation; vessel no longer at least five
net tons; vessel no longer capable of transportation.

Cancellation   1. Certificate of documentation

III. Additional Requirements for Specially Qualified Vessels

Type Vessel	Initial or Subsequent Application	Requirements
Captured or Forfeited	Initial	1. Application form (CG-1258) 2. Citizenship declaration (MA-899) 3. Marking evidence (CG-1322) 4. Recording fee 5. Tonnage evidence (CG-5397)

		6. Title evidence (court)
		7. Owner citizenship (since court)
	Subsequent	1-4. Same as Initial 1-4
		5. Title evidence (court)
Special Legislation	Initial	1-5. Same as Captured Initial 1-5
		6. Copy of last flagging action
		7. Title evidence since last flag
		8. Citizenship evidence since flag
		9. Evidence of removal from foreign registry
	Subsequent	1-4. Same as Captured Initial 1-4
		5. Title evidence since flagged
		6. Evidence of removal from foreign registry
Wrecked	Initial	1-5. Same as Captured Initial 1-5
		6. Title evidence since administrative determination
		7. Citizenship evidence since administrative determination
	Subsequent	1-6. Same as Wrecked Initial 1-6

IV. Hints When Buying and Selling

In order to verify the status of the vessel's title, a copy of the abstract of title (CG-1332), as well as a certificate of ownership (CG-1330) setting forth ownership and encumbrances, can be obtained directly from the seller's documentation office. These are information copies, which can't be used to change home ports. If the boat was previously documented at a port of documentation different from the buyer's, the seller should ask his documentation office to forward an official abstract of title to the buyer's documentation office. This is the only way the Coast Guard will change home ports.

In case the seller will be difficult to contact after the sale, it would be wise to obtain the Coast Guard's mortgagee consent form (CG-4593), if applicable, and the bill-of-sale form (CG-1340), in time to get the seller's signature and a notarization.

Examination Subjects for U.S. Coast Guard Licenses

This table was extracted from Table 10.910-2, Subjects for Deck Licenses; 46 CFR 10.910; as presented in Vol. 52, No. 200, of the Federal Register, and updated. For a current listing, see 46 CFR Part 10, or contact a Coast Guard regional examination center or a Coast Guard license prep school.

Column 1 = Master or mate, near coastal, 0-200 gross tons. Includes master, near coastal, 100 tons.
Column 2 = Operator, OUPV (six-pack), near coastal.
Column 3 = Operator, OUPV (six-pack), inland.
Column 4 = Master or mate, Great Lakes/Inland, 0-200 gross tons. Includes master, inland, 100 gross tons.

Note: An "X" in table denotes exam subject. A number refers to note at end of table.

SUBJECT	1	2	3	4
NAVIGATION				
Piloting	X	X	X	X
Chart navigation	X	X	X	X
Restricted visibility	X	X	X	X
Traffic separation schemes	X	X		
Aids to navigation	X	X	X	X
Charts, navigational publications, and Notices to Mariners	X	X	X	X
Distance off	X	X	X	X
Bearing problems	X	X		X
Fix or running fix	X	X	X	X
Electronic navigation	X			X
Instruments and accessories	X	X	X	X
MARLINSPIKE SEAMANSHIP AND PURCHASES	X	X	X	X
WATCHKEEPING				
COLREGS (International Rules)	X	X	1	1

	1	2	3	4
Inland Navigational Rules	X	X	X	X
Watchkeeping	X			X
Navigation Safety Regs 33 CFR 164	X	X	X	X
COMPASS—MAGNETIC AND GYRO				
Principles of magnetic & gyro compass	X	2	2	2
Magnetic & gyro compass error/correction	X	X	X	X
METEOROLOGY AND OCEANOGRAPHY				
Characteristics of weather systems	X	X	X	X
Tide and current publications	X	X	X	X
Tide and current calculations	X	X		X
SHIP MANEUVERING AND HANDLING				
Shiphandling in rivers/estuaries	X	X	X	X
Maneuvering in shallow water	X	X	X	X
Interaction with bank/passing ship	X	X	X	X
Berthing and unberthing	X	X	X	X
Anchoring and mooring	X	X	X	X
Dragging, clearing fouled anchors	X			X
Heavy weather ship/aircraft/tow	X	X	X	X
Heavy weather, lifeboats/rafts	X			
Wake reduction		X	X	
Towing operations	X	X	X	X
SHIP STABILITY, CONSTRUCTION, AND DAMAGE CONTROL				
Trim and stability	X			X
Damage trim and stability	3			
Stability, trim, stress calculation	3			
Vessel structural members	3			X
Damage control	3			X
SHIP POWER PLANTS				
Marine power plant principles	3			X
Marine engineering terms	3			X
Small engine operations and maintenance	X	X	X	X
CARGO HANDLING AND STOWAGE				
Cargo stowage & security	X			X
FIRE PREVENTION AND FIREFIGHTING APPLIANCES				
Organization of fire drills	X			X
Classes and chemistry of fire	X	X	X	X
Firefighting systems	X			X
Firefighting equipment & regulations	3			3
Firefighting equipment for T-boats	X			X
Basic firefighting & prevention	X	X	X	X
EMERGENCY PROCEDURES				
Collision	X	X	X	X

Subject				
Temporary repairs	X	X	X	X
Passenger/crew safety in emergency	X	X	X	X
Fire or explosion	X	X	X	X
Abandon ship	X	X	X	X
Rescuing survivors	X			X
Man overboard	X	X	X	X
MEDICAL CARE				
First aid	X	X	X	X
MARITIME LAW				
SOLAS	3			
Load Lines				3
Certification & documentation of vessels	X	X	X	3
Ship sanitation	X	X	X	X
Rules & regs for vessel inspection	3			3
Rules & regs for T-boat nspection	X			X
Rules & regs for uninspected vessels	X	X	X	
Pollution prevention regs	X	X	X	X
COLREG responsibilities	3	3		3
Pilotage	X			
Licensing & certification of seamen	X	X	X	
Shipment & discharge, manning	X			
COMMUNICATIONS				
Radiotelephone communications	X	X	X	X
Signals: storm/wreck/distress/special	X	X	X	X
LIFESAVING				
Lifesaving appliance regulations	3			3
Lifesaving appliance operations for T-boats	X			X
Lifesaving appliance operation	3			3
Lifesaving appliance regulations for T-boats	X			X
SAIL/AUXILIARY SAIL ENDORSEMENT	4	4	4	4

Notes

1. Exam includes COLREGS unless license is to be limited to non-COLREGS waters.

2. Magnetic only.

3. For licenses over one hundred gross tons.

4. The following subjects are in addition to subjects covered in the basic license: Sail vessel safety precautions, Rules of the Road, operations, heavy-weather procedures, navigation, maneuvering, and sailing terminology.

Government Publications for Charter Operators

For pamphlets prepared by SCORE (Service Corps of Retired Executives), and provided through the U.S. Small Business Administration (SBA), see section I below. Section II lists SBA booklets on sale through the Government Printing Office (GPO). Section III contains a listing of books relating to U.S. Coast Guard subjects. They are also available from the GPO.

I. Pamphlets Prepared by SCORE

When this book went to press, the following Management Aid (MA) pamphlets were being provided at no charge, except for handling costs, by the SBA. They are representative of types of material that can be helpful to charter operators. For an updated list, obtain a copy of SBA 115A, Business Development Pamphlets, from the local SBA or SCORE office, or contact: U.S. Small Business Administration, P.O. Box 30, Denver, CO 80201-0030.

Financial Management and Analysis
MA 1.001	*The ABC's of Borrowing*
MA 1.004	*Basic Budgets for Profit Planning*
MA 1.009	*A Venture Capital Primer for Small Business*
MA 1.010	*Accounting Services for Small Service Firms*
MA 1.011	*Analyze Your Records to Reduce Costs*
MA 1.015	*Budgeting in a Small Service Firm*
MA 1.016	*Sound Cash Management and Borrowing*
MA 1.017	*Keeping Records in Small Business*
MA 1.018	*Checklist for Profit Watching*
MA 1.019	*Simple Breakeven Analysis for Small Stores*
MA 4.013	*A Pricing Checklist for Small Retailers*

General Management and Planning
MA 2.002	*Locating or Relocating Your Business*
MA 2.004	*Problems in Managing a Family-Owned Business*
MA 2.010	*Planning and Goal Setting for Small Business*
MA 2.014	*Should You Lease or Buy Equipment?*

MA 2.016	*Checklist for Going Into Business*
MA 2.020	*Business Plan for Retailers*
MA 2.022	*Business Plan for Small Service Firms*
MA 2.025	*Thinking About Going into Business?*
MA 2.026	*Feasibility Checklist for Starting a Small Business of Your Own*
MA 2.027	*How to Get Started with a Small Business Computer*
MA 2.028	*The Business Plan for Homebased Business*
MA 3.005	*Stock Control for Small Stores*
MA 3.006	*Reducing Shoplifting Losses*
MA 3.010	*Techniques for Problem Solving*
MA 5.005	*Preventing Employee Pilferage*

Marketing

MA 4.002	*Creative Selling: The Competitive Edge*
MA 4.012	*Marketing Checklist for Small Retailers*
MA 4.015	*Advertising Guidelines for Small Retail Firms*
MA 4.018	*Plan Your Advertising Budget*
MA 4.019	*Learning About Your Market*

Personnel Management

MA 5.001	*Checklist for Developing a Training Program*
MA 5.007	*Staffing Your Store*
MA 5.008	*Managing Employee Benefits*

Miscellaneous

| SBB 2 | *Home Businesses* (a bibliography) |

II. Small Business Administration (SBA) Booklets

When this book went to press, the following SBA booklets were being sold by the Government Printing Office. They are representative of the types of material that can be helpful to charter operators. For an updated list with current prices, obtain a copy of SBA 115B from the local SBA office, or write: Superintendent of Documents, Government Printing Office, Washington, D.C. 20402; or call (202) 783-3238. The GPO will take telephone orders from 8:00 A.M. to 4:00 P.M. (Eastern time), Monday through Friday (except holidays). VISA, MasterCard, CHOICE, and GPO Deposit Accounts are acceptable.

Small Business Management Series—Specific Management Techniques

1.	*An Employee Suggestion System for Small Companies*
15.	*Handbook of Small Business Finance*
20.	*Ratio Analysis for Small Business*

25.	*Guides for Profit Planning*
27.	*Profitable Community Relations for Small Business*
30.	*Insurance and Risk Management for Small Business*
31.	*Management Audit for Small Retailers*
32.	*Financial Recordkeeping for Small Stores*
33.	*Small Store Planning for Growth*
38.	*Management Audit for Small Service Firms*
41.	*Purchasing Management and Inventory Control for Small Business*
42.	*Managing the Small Service Firm for Growth and Profit*
43.	*Credit and Collections for Small Stores*

Starting and Managing Series—"Look Before Leaping"

1.	*Starting and Managing a Small Business of Your Own*
101.	*Starting and Managing a Small Service Firm*

Business Basics—Self-Study Booklets with Texts and Questions

1001	*The Profit Plan*
1002	*Capital Planning*
1003	*Understanding Money Sources*
1004	*Evaluating Money Sources*
1005	*Asset Management*
1006	*Managing Fixed Assets*
1007	*Understanding Costs*
1008	*Cost Control*
1009	*Marketing Strategy*
1010	*Retail Buying Function*
1011	*Inventory Management—Wholesale/Retail*
1012	*Retail Merchandise Management*
1013	*Consumer Credit*
1014	*Credit and Collections: Policy and Procedures*
1018	*Risk Management and Insurance*
1019	*Managing Retail Salespeople*
1020	*Job Analysis, Job Specifications, and Job Descriptions*
1021	*Recruiting and Selecting Employees*
1022	*Training and Developing Employees*
1023	*Employee Relations and Personnel Policies*

III. U.S. Coast Guard–Related Publications

When this book went to press, the publications in this appendix were available from the Government Printing Office (GPO) at the prices indicated. Current editions can be obtained by writing: Superintendent of Documents, Government

Printing Office, Washington, D.C. 20402; or by calling (202) 783-3238. The GPO will take telephone orders from 8:00 A.M. to 4:00 P.M. (Eastern time), Monday through Friday (except holidays). VISA, MasterCard, CHOICE, and GPO Deposit Accounts are acceptable.

Pollution, Marine Sanitation Regulations: 33 CFR Parts 1-199, $27.00.

Safety, Boarding, Licensing, Manning, Uninspected Vessels, Tank Vessels: 46 CFR Parts 1-40, $13.00.

Load Lines, Documentation, Admeasurement: 46 CFR Parts 41-69, $13.00.

Passenger Vessels: 46 CFR Parts 70-89, $7.00.

Subdivision, Stability, Small Passenger Vessels: 46 CFR 166-199, $13.00.

Navigational Rules, Inland and International (Rules of the Road): M16672.2A, $7.50.

Marine Fire Prevention, Firefighting and Fire Safety: 181-783.64601, $14.00.

U.S. Customs Regulations: 19 CFR Parts 1-199, $14.00

Federal Communications Regulations: 47 CFR Part 30-End, $20.00.

Inspection and Certification Checklist

This is a sample list. Requirements could vary. Refer to 46 CFR Part T, located in 46 CFR 166-199, for specifics.

1. Submit application (CG-3752).

2. Dry-dock vessel for USCG examination at a mutually agreed time and place.

3. Submit plans, blueprints, or sketches of vessel and systems. Include listing and description of all basic machinery and electrical equipment.

4. Provide two means of access or emergency escape to all compartments over 12 feet in length.

5. Provide adequate ventilation to all closed spaces.

6. Provide fume-tight separation of machinery and fuel-tank spaces from accommodation spaces.

7. For vessels that fish exclusively, provide rails with maximum 12-inch spacing of courses at periphery of all decks accessible to passengers. For excursion vessels, fill in the rails completely.

8. Provide guards over all exposed moving machinery.

9. Provide freeing ports for well decks and/or scuppers for cockpits.

10. Provide a collision bulkhead.

11. Provide watertight bulkheads with one compartment subdivision if more than forty-nine passengers are to be carried.

12. Provide stability data.

13. Provide watertight hatches or 12-inch trunks, and 6-inch or 3-inch door coamings at weather-deck openings in deckhouse.

14. Provide sea valves at all hull penetrations within 6 inches of waterline and below, and reach rods where needed for accessibility.

15. Provide USCG-approved life floats or buoyant apparatus for route and service intended.

16. Remove unapproved or unmaintained lifesaving gear from the vessel.

17. Provide water lights and manila painter (24 feet by 2 inches) or its equivalent for buoyant apparatus; also provide two paddles for life floats if carried.

18. Provide one approved-type life preserver for each person on board, and an additional 10 percent of the total in child's life preservers.

19. Provide topside stowage for life preservers, well marked if not readily visible, with child's life preservers stowed separately.

20. Provide an appropriate number of approved-type 24-inch ring buoys, with water, light, and 60 feet of line.

21. Provide six red and six orange hand-held flares, or 12 hand-held combination flare-and-smoke distress signals of approved type and current date.

22. Provide a portable watertight container for flares.

23. Provide a portable 5 GPM (minimum) fire pump.

24. Provide an installed CO_2 system for the machinery and fuel-tank spaces if using gasoline.

25. Provide one B-I extinguisher for wheelhouse, one B-I extinguisher for gasoline machinery spaces, two B-II extinguishers for diesel machinery spaces without installed CO_2 systems, one B-II extinguisher for each accommodation and/or galley space—all to be of USCG or UL marine approved type.

26. Remount all electric motors, switches, wiring, and other potential spark-producers as high above the bilges as practicable.

27. Provide approved backfire traps, and drip pans with flameproof screens under updraft carburetors and filters of all gasoline machinery.

28. Provide metal marine-type strainers for gasoline lines. Strainers must be of the type that opens on top for cleaning screens. A drip pan fitted with flame screen must be installed under the strainer.

29. Provide suitable insulation and/or coolant for exhaust pipes.

30. Install suitable fuel tanks, or provide data and prove existing tanks to be in reasonable compliance for fuel used and amount carried.

31. Provide 1 1/2-inch diameter, electrically bonded fuel fill pipes, rigged to permit sounding of tanks and prevent an overflow of liquid or vapor from entering the inside of the vessel.

32. Provide vent lines for fuel tanks, to be of 3/4-inch O.D. tube minimum for gasoline, and no less than 5/8-inch O.D. tube for diesel tanks.

33. Provide marked emergency shutoff valves at fuel tanks, operable from the weather deck.

34. Provide fuel flex lines or loops at engines.

35. Permanently seal closed all means of drawing gasoline below deck; provide a plugged or capped valve at all diesel water traps or strainers to prevent fuel leakage.

36. Remove all petcocks from diesel and gasoline fuel systems. Provide metal-seating screw-down valves.

37. Provide 30-by-30-mesh-per-inch flameproof screens at fuel-tank vents.

38. Prior to installation, fuel tanks vented to the atmosphere must be tested

to and withstand a pressure of 5 psi or one and a half times the maximum head to which they may be subjected in service, whichever is greater.

39. Provide a bilge suction system, with separate lines, check valves, and strainers for each watertight compartment. Operating valves are to be centrally grouped or manifolded and readily accessible.

40. Provide an accessible valve aft of the collision bulkhead at bilge-line penetration.

41. Provide a bilge pump in accordance with 46 CFR Table 182.25-10 (a).

42. Provide an emergency hand tiller for single-screw vessels.

43. Provide an interlocked ignition and vent-exhaust blower switch for each gasoline engine.

44. Provide lead- or plastic-lined battery boxes for batteries, at least 10-inch headroom, checked to prevent shifting of batteries, effectively screened or boxed if in same compartment with gasoline machinery, and well vented.

45. All connections must be made to the battery terminals with permanent type connections.

46. Provide National Electric Code type accessories, such as fuses, switches, and sockets; to be listed or equivalent to UL types.

47. Remove all dead and unused wire. All wiring smaller than #14 AWG must be removed from the vessel.

48. Provide junction boxes for all wire splices not made in fixtures or switch panels.

49. Provide an electrical bonding or grounding system joining all major metal components of the vessel, including fuel tanks, lines, electrical motors, radio, ground-plate, engine, and rudder stock.

50. The electrical system must be either over 50 volts or under 50 volts.

51. Remove all liquefied petroleum fuel or gasoline heating and cooking fixtures from the vessel.

52. Provide navigation lights and shapes, whistles, foghorns, and fog bells as required by the applicable Rules of the Road.

53. Provide adequate ground tackle.

54. Provide a suitable compass.

55. Provide a radiotelephone, with current FCC station and personnel licenses.

56. Provide emergency lighting by fixed or portable battery lamps.

57. Post emergency instructions.

58. Post operator licenses and certificates of inspection under glass in a place accessible to passengers. Ensure that certification expiration-date stickers are properly posted.

59. Attach retroreflective material to life jackets, and provide lights if route is over twenty miles from a harbor of safe refuge.

60. Any vessel fitted with a toilet is required to have an approved Marine Sanitation Device.

61. Have onboard vessel documentation with service of vessel showing passengers, or certificate of numbers if vessel is under five net tons.

62. Provide emergency position-indicating radio beacon (EPIRB) for vessels in ocean and coastwise service.

63. Provide a fire ax if vessel is over 65 feet in length.

64. Provide adequate and up-to-date charts for areas of operation.

65. Adequately mark the hull, lifesaving gear, emergency escapes, and fuel shutoff valves.

Loans—How to Apply for a Small Business Administration Loan

These guidelines contain the basic package needed for any small-business loan application. They were prepared by SCORE, Suncoast/Pinellas Chapter #115, with addresses at 300 East Building, Suite 525, 300 31st Street North, St. Petersburg, Florida 33713 (tel. 813-327-7207); and Southeast Bank Building, Suite 505, 801 West Bay Drive, Largo, Florida 33540 (tel. 813-585-4571). The guidelines include the caveat: "In a city of over 200,000 population, a person must be turned down by two banks before applying for an SBA loan."

For New Businesses

1. Describe in detail the type of business to be established.

2. List your business education, experience, and management capabilities.

3. Prepare an estimate of how much you or others have to invest in the business and how much you will need to borrow.

4. Prepare a current, signed personal financial statement of the owner(s).

5. Prepare a projected profit-and-loss statement for the first year the business will operate.

6. List collateral to be offered as security for the loan. List the market value of each item.

7. Take this material with you and see your banker. Ask for a direct bank loan; if declined, ask the bank to make the loan under SBA's loan-guaranty plan. If the bank is interested in an SBA guaranty loan, ask the banker to contact SBA for discussion of your application. In most cases of guaranty loans, SBA will deal directly with the bank.

8. If a guaranty loan is not available, send the first six items to the nearest SBA office.

For Established Businesses

1. Prepare a currently dated, signed balance sheet listing all assets and all liabilities of the business. Do not include personal items.

2. Prepare a signed profit-and-loss statement for the previous full year and for the current period to the date of the balance sheet.

3. Prepare a current, signed, personal financial statement of the owner(s).

4. List collateral to be offered as security for the loan. List the market value of each item.

5. State the amount of the loan requested and explain the exact purpose for which it will be used.

6. Take this material with you and see your banker. Ask for a direct bank loan; if declined, ask the bank to make the loan under SBA's loan-guaranty plan. If the bank is interested in an SBA guaranty loan, ask the banker to contact SBA for discussion of your application. In most cases of guaranty loans, SBA will deal directly with the bank.

7. If a guaranty loan is not available, send the first five items to the nearest SBA office.

Suspension and Revocation Guidelines for Administrative Law Judges

This table, published in Part 5 of 46 CFR, expresses a range considered appropriate for a particular act or offense prior to the judge's considering matters in mitigation or aggravation, or considering whether the respondent is a repeat offender.

Type of Offense	*Range of Order (suspension, in months, or revocation)*
Misconduct	
Failure to obey master's/ ship officer's order	1-3
Failure to comply with U.S. law or regulations	1-3
Possession of intoxicating liquor	1-4
Failure to obey master's written instructions	2-4
Improper performance of duties related to vessel safety	2-5
Failure to join vessel (required crew member)	2-6
Violent acts against other persons (without injury)	2-6
Failure to perform duties relating to vessel safety	3-6
Theft	3-6
Violent acts against other persons (injury)	4-revocation
Use, possession, or sale of dangerous drugs	revocation

Negligence

    Negligently performing
        duties related to vessel
        navigation   2-6

    Negligently performing
        nonnavigational duties
        related to vessel safety   1-3

    Neglect of vessel navigation
        duties   3-6

    Neglect of nonnavigational
        safety-related duties   2-4

Incompetence   "The only proper order is
                           revocation."

Dangerous drugs (46 U.S.C. 7704) "The only proper order is
                           revocation."

U.S. Coast Guard Addresses

Part I lists district offices. Part II shows documentation offices. Part III contains a listing of marine safety offices, marine inspection offices, marine safety detachments, and marine inspection detachments. Part IV lists regional examination centers.

I. Coast Guard District Offices

Commander
1st Coast Guard District
408 Atlantic Ave.
Boston, MA 02210

Commander
2nd Coast Guard District
1430 Olive St.
St. Louis, MO 63103

Commander
5th Coast Guard District
431 Crawford St.
Portsmouth, VA 23705

Commander
7th Coast Guard District
Bricknell Plaza Building
909 S.E. 1st Ave.
Miami, FL 33131

Commander
8th Coast Guard District
500 Camp St.
New Orleans, LA 70130

Commander
9th Coast Guard District
1240 E. 9th St.
Cleveland, OH 44199

Commander
11th Coast Guard District
400 Oceangate Blvd.
Long Beach, CA 90882

Commander
13th Coast Guard District
915 2nd Ave.
Seattle, WA 91874

Commander
14th Coast Guard District
300 Ala Moana Blvd.
Honolulu, HI 96813

Commander
17th Coast Guard District
P.O. Box 3-5000
Juneau, AK 99801

II. Coast Guard Documentation Offices

Write to: U.S. Coast Guard, Documentation Officer, and complete the address with the office desired.

447 Commercial St.
Boston, MA 02109

601 Rockwell Ave., Room 455
Cleveland, OH 44114

433 Ala Moana Blvd., Room 1
Honolulu, HI 96813

7300 Wingate St., Room 326
Houston, TX 77011

612 Willoughby Ave.
Juneau, AK 99801

165 N. Pico Ave.
Long Beach, CA 90802

155 S. Miami Ave.
Miami, FL 33130

F. Edward Hebert Bldg.
600 S. Maestri Pl.
New Orleans, LA 70130

Battery Park Bldg.
New York, NY 10004

Federal Bldg.
200 Granby Mall
Norfolk, VA 23510

U.S. Custom House, Rm. 805
Philadelphia, PA 19106

6767 N. Basin Ave.
Portland, OR 97217

210 N. Tucker Blvd., Rm. 1128
St. Louis, MO 63101

Bldg. 14, Rm. 128
Government Island
Alameda, CA 94501

1519 Alaskan Way S., Bldg. 1
Seattle, WA 98134

III. Coast Guard Marine Safety Offices, Marine Inspection Offices, Marine Safety Detachments, and Marine Inspection Detachments

The activity nearest the vessel's port should be contacted for purposes of marine inspections.

Supervisor
USCG Marine Safety Detachment
CG Supt. Cntr., P.O. Box 5A
Kodiak, AK 99619-5000

Supervisor
USCG Marine Safety Detachment
Rm. 202, 329 Harbor Dr., Lloyd Ctr.
Sitka, AK 99835-7554

Commanding Officer
USCG Marine Safety Office
701 C St., Box 17
Anchorage, AK 99513-0065

Commanding Officer
USCG Marine Safety Office
612 Willoughby Ave.
Juneau, AK 99801-1732

Commanding Officer
USCG Marine Safety Office
P.O. Box 486
Valdez, AK 99686-0486

Supervisor
USCG Marine Safety Detachment
Rm. 306, 402 Lee St.
Decatur, AL 35601-1855

Commanding Officer
USCG Marine Safety Office
1900 1st Natl. Bank Bldg., Box 2924
Mobile, AL 36652-2924

Supervisor
USCG Marine Safety Detachment
Bldg. 188, NAVWPNSTA
Concord, CA 94520-0001

Supervisor
USCG Marine Safety Detachment
Cdr. Marianas Sect., Box 176
FPO San Francisco, CA 96630

Supervisor
USCG Marine Safety Detachment
111 Harbor Way
Santa Barbara, CA 93109-2315

Commanding Officer
USCG Marine Safety Office
Bldg. 14, Coast Guard Island
Alameda, CA 94501-5100

Commanding Officer
USCG Marine Safety Office
165 N. Pico Ave.
Long Beach, CA 90802-1096

Commanding Officer
USCG Marine Safety Office
2710 Harbor Dr. N.
San Diego, CA 92101-1064

Supervisor
USCG Marine Inspection
Detachment
Rm. 6, Custom House, 150 Bank St.
New London, CT 06320-6084

Supervisor
USCG Marine Safety Detachment
Fed. Bldg. Rm. 204
301 Simonton St.
Key West, FL 33040-6812

Commanding Officer
USCG Marine Safety Office
Justice Bldg., 155 S. Miami Ave.
Miami, FL 33130-1609

Commanding Officer
USCG Marine Safety Office
Rm. 213, Talleyrand Ave.
Jacksonville, FL 32206-3497

Commanding Officer
USCG Marine Safety Office
155 Columbia Dr.
Tampa, FL 33606-3598

Commanding Officer
USCG Marine Safety Office
P.O. Box 8191
Savannah, GA 31402-8191

Commanding Officer
USCG Marine Safety Office
433 Ala Moana Blvd., Rm. 1
Honolulu, HI 96813-4909

Supervisor
USCG Marine Safety Detachment
Rm. 332 Fed. Office Bldg.
131 E. 4th St.
Davenport, IA 52801-1513

Supervisor
USCG Marine Safety Detachment
Foot of Washington St.
East Peoria, IL 61611-2039

Commanding Officer
USCG Marine Safety Office
610 S. Canal St.
Chicago, IL 60607-4573

Supervisor
USCG Marine Safety Detachment
P.O. Box 3391
Evansville, IN 47732-3391

Commanding Officer
USCG Marine Safety Office
600 Federal Pl., Rm. 360
Louisville, KY 40202-2230

Commanding Officer
USCG Marine Safety Office
P.O. Box 7509
Paducah, KY 42002-7509

Supervisor
USCG Marine Inspection
Detachment
626 Main St.
Baton Rouge, LA 70801-1999

Supervisor
USCG Marine Inspection
Detachment
P.O. Box 989
Houma, LA 70360-0989

Supervisor
USCG Marine Safety Detachment
Port of Lake Charles, 150 Marine
Lake Charles, LA 70601-5612

Commanding Officer
USCG Marine Safety Office
Hebert Bldg, 600 S. Maestri Pl.
New Orleans, LA 70130-3476

Commanding Officer
USCG Marine Safety Office
P.O. Box 2374
Morgan City, LA 70280-2374

Supervisor
USCG Marine Safety Detachment
Mary Dunn Rd., Barnstable Airport
Hyannis, MA 02601-1995

Commanding Officer
USCG Marine Safety Office
447 Commercial St.
Boston, MA 02109-1086

Commanding Officer
USCG Marine Safety Office
U.S. Custom House
Baltimore, MD 21202-4022

Supervisor
USCG Marine Safety Detachment
871 Hammond St.
Bangor, ME 04401-4303

Commanding Officer
USCG Marine Safety Office
P.O. Box 108
Portland, ME 04112-0108

Commanding Officer
USCG Marine Inspection Office
Municipal Bldg.
St. Ignace, MI 49781-1425

Commanding Officer
USCG Marine Safety Office
2660 E. Atwater St.
Detroit, MI 48207-4418

Supervisor
USCG Marine Safety Detachment
P.O. Box 65428
St. Paul, MN 55165-0428

Commanding Officer
USCG Marine Safety Office
Canal Park
Duluth, MN 55802-2352

Commanding Officer
USCG Marine Safety Office
P.O. Box D-17
St. Louis, MO 63188-0017

Supervisor
USCG Marine Safety Detachment
P.O. Box 882
Greenville, MS 38701-0882

Supervisor
USCG Marine Safety Detachment
Rm. 126 Maritime Bldg.
113 Arendell
Morehead City, NC 28557-4248

Commanding Officer
USCG Marine Safety Office
Suite 500, 272 N. Front St.
Wilmington, NC 28401-3907

Commanding Officer
USCG Marine Inspection Office
Battery Park Bldg.
New York, NY 10004-1466

Supervisor
USCG Marine Safety Detachment
P.O. Box 1886
Alexandria Bay, NY 13607-1086

Commanding Officer
USCG Marine Safety Office
Rm. 1111 Fed. Bldg.
111 W. Huron St.
Buffalo, NY 14202-2395

Supervisor
USCG Marine Safety Detachment
4335 River Rd.
Cincinnati, OH 45204-1094

Supervisor
USCG Marine Safety Detachment
P.O. Box 129
Marietta, OH 45750-0129

Commanding Officer
USCG Marine Safety Office
Fed. Bldg. Rm. 101, 234 Summit St.
Toledo, OH 43604-1590

Commanding Officer
USCG Marine Safety Office
1055 E. Ninth St.
Cleveland, OH 44104-1092

Commanding Officer
USCG Marine Safety Office
6767 N. Basin Ave.
Portland, OR 97217-3929

Commanding Officer
USCG Marine Inspection Office
801 Custom House
Philadelphia, PA 19106-2974

Commanding Officer
USCG Marine Safety Office
700 Kossman Bldg.
Forbes & Stanwix
Pittsburgh, PA 15222-1371

Supervisor
USCG Marine Safety Detachment
P.O. Box 34, Playa Station
Port Ponce, PR 00734-3034

Commanding Officer
USCG Marine Safety Office
P.O. Box S-3666
Old San Juan, PR 00904-3666

Commanding Officer
USCG Marine Safety Office
John O'Pastore Federal Building
Providence, RI 02903-1790

Commanding Officer
USCG Marine Safety Office
P.O. Box 724, 196 Tradd St.
Charleston, SC 29401-1899

Commanding Officer
USCG Marine Safety Office
A-935 Court House Annex
110 9th Ave. S.
Nashville, TN 37203-3817

Commanding Officer
USCG Marine Safety Office
100 N. Main St., Suite 1134
Memphis, TN 38103-5014

Commanding Officer
USCG Marine Inspection Office
8876 Gulf Freeway, Suite 210
Houston, TX 77017-6595

Supervisor
USCG Marine Safety Detachment
Box 2, Star Route
Brownsville, TX 78521-9217

Commanding Officer
USCG Marine Safety Office
Fed. BLdg., 2875 75th St. & Hy. 69
Port Arthur, TX 77640-2099

Commanding Officer
USCG Marine Safety Office
Room 301, Post Office Bldg.
601 Rosenberg
Galveston, TX 77550-1705

Commanding Officer
USCG Marine Safety Office
P.O. Box 1621
Corpus Christi, TX 78403-1621

Commanding Officer
USCG Marine Safety Office
Fed. Bldg., 200 Granby Mall
Norfolk, VA 23510-1888

Supervisor
USCG Marine Safety Detachment
P.O. Box 818
St. Thomas, VI 00801-0818

Supervisor
USCG Marine Safety Detachment
P.O. Box 291
Anacortes, WA 98221

Commanding Officer
USCG Marine Safety Office
1519 Alaskan Way S., Bldg. 1
Seattle, WA 98134-1192

Commanding Officer
USCG Marine Inspection Office
360 Louisiana St.
Sturgeon Bay, WI 54235-2479

Commanding Officer
USCG Marine Safety Office
2420 S. Lincoln Memorial Dr.
Milwaukee, WI 53207-1997

Commanding Officer
USCG Marine Safety Office
P.O. Box 2412
Huntington, WV 25725-2412

IV. Coast Guard Regional Examination Centers

Regional Examination Center
USCG Marine Safety Office
612 Willoughby Ave.
Juneau, AK 99801
(907) 586-7325

Regional Examination Center
USCG Marine Safety Office
701 C St., Box 17
Anchorage, AK 99513
(907) 271-5137

Regional Examination Center
USCG Marine Safety Office
165 N. Pico Ave.
Long Beach, CA 90802
(213) 590-2383

Regional Examination Center
USCG Marine Inspection Office
Battery Park Bldg.
New York, NY 10004
(212) 668-7864

Regional Examination Center
USCG Marine Safety Office
Bldg. 14, Rm. 109, Govt. Island
Alameda, CA 94501
(415) 437-3094

Regional Examination Center
USCG Marine Safety Office
RM. 501 Fed. Bldg., 234 Summit St.
Toledo, OH 43604
(419) 259-6394

Regional Examination Center
USCG Marine Safety Office
Justice Bldg., 155 S. Miami Ave.
Miami, FL 33130
(305) 536-6874

Regional Examination Center
USCG Marine Safety Office
6767 N. Basin Ave.
Portland, OR 97217
(503) 240-9346

Regional Examination Center
USCG Marine Safety Office
433 Ala Moana Blvd., Rm. 1
Honolulu, HI 96813
(808) 546-7318

Regional Examination Center
USCG Marine Safety Office
P.O. Box S-3666
Old San Juan, PR 00904
(809) 725-0857

Regional Examination Center
USCG Marine Safety Office
Hebert Bldg., 600 S. Maestri Pl.
New Orleans, LA 70130
(504) 589-6183

Regional Examination Center
USCG Marine Safety Office
P.O. Box 724, 196 Tradd St.
Charleston, SC 29401-1899
(803) 724-4394

Regional Examination Center
USCG Marine Safety Office
447 Commercial St.
Boston, MA 02109-1086
(617) 523-0139

Regional Examination Center
USCG Marine Safety Office
100 N. Main St., Suite 1134
Memphis, TN 38103
(901) 521-3297

Regional Examination Center
USCG Marine Safety Office
U.S. Custom House
Baltimore, MD 21202
(301) 962-5134

Regional Examination Center
USCG Marine Inspection Office
8876 Gulf Freeway
Houston, TX 77017
(713) 229-3559

Regional Examination Center
USCG Marine Safety Office
210 N. Tucker Blvd., Rm. 1128
St. Louis, MO 63101
(314) 425-4657

Regional Monitoring Station
USCG Marine Safety Office
Fed. Bldg., 200 Granby Mall
Norfolk, VA 23510
Call Baltimore Center

Regional Examination Center
USCG Marine Safety Office
1519 Alaskan Way S., Bldg. 1
Seattle, WA 98134
(206) 286-5510

Notes

1. Making a Business of Boating

1. Information from "Liveaboard Charter Operators Blend Business With Pleasure," by Jane Eagleson, *Soundings,* Pratt Street, Essex, Connecticut 06426, October 1987; and from telephone conversation with Terri and Jeff Siben.

2. Information taken from article "Say Goodby to the Office," by Sid Stapleton, *Motor Boating & Sailing,* May 1987, 224 West 57th Street, New York, New York 10019.

3. "Retail Dive Store: Management and Operations," Member Price List, Product #70193, $69.95, from Professional Association of Diving Instructors (PADI), 1251 East Dyer Road, Suite 100, Santa Ana, California 92705-5605. Information provided by C. K. Stewart, director of marketing.

4. Information from "Developer Gambling on Turning Oil Rigs Into Floating Casinos," by Jim Flannery, *Soundings,* Pratt Street, Essex, Connecticut 06426, October 1987.

2. Yacht Management

1. Information for this section was compiled and summarized from brochures obtained from five major yacht-management firms. Company names have not been mentioned because each program represents only a portion of the companies' total packages, so comparisons could be misleading.

3. Starting Your Business

1. SBA MA 2.016: *Checklist for Going Into Business.*

2. SBA MA 2.025: *Thinking About Going Into Business?*

3. See chapter on the marketing plan for information about the business plan. Also see SBA MA 2.022: *Business Plan for Small Service Firms,* and SBA MA 2.020: *Business Plan for Retailers.*

4. IRS Publication 334: *Tax Guide For Small Businesses,* 1986, chapter 28.

5. Ibid.

6. IRS Publication 542: *Tax Information on Corporations,* 1986, "Forming a Corporation."

4. Obtaining a Loan

1. This chapter draws upon portions of two SBA publications—MA 1.001: *The ABC's of Borrowing*, and MA 1.016: *Sound Cash Management and Borrowing*.

2. SBA MA 1.016: *Sound Cash Management and Borrowing*, by John F. Murphy, retired bank executive and member of Manasota SCORE chapter, Sarasota, Florida.

3. SBA MA 1.009: *A Venture Capital Primer for Small Business*, by LaRue Tone Hosmer, University of Michigan, Ann Arbor.

5. Accounting and Budgeting

1. For full details of tax years and tax accounting methods, see current version of IRS Publication 334: *Tax Guide for Small Businesses*.

2. IRS Publication 334 (rev. Nov. 1988), chapter 4.

3. IRS Publication 583 (rev. Nov. 1988), *Information for Business Taxpayers*.

4. This section relies greatly upon SBA MA 1.011: *Analyze Your Records to Reduce Costs*, by Alfred B. Abraham, CPA, managing director, Business Diagnostics, New York, New York.

5. SBA MA 1.010: *Accounting Services for Small Service Firms*, by Irving M. Cooper, member of Cooper, Weinstein and Kumin, Certified Public Accountants, Worcester, Massachusetts.

6. SBA MA 1.011.

7. Ibid.

8. This section extracts information from SBA MA 1.015: *Budgeting in a Small Service Firm*, by Phyllis A. Barker, assistant professor of accounting, Indiana State University, Terre Haute, Indiana.

9. SBA MA 1.016: *Sound Cash Management and Borrowing*, by John F. Murphy, retired bank executive and member of Manasota SCORE chapter, Sarasota, Florida.

10. See SBA MA 1.004: *Basic Budgets for Profit Planning*, by Charles J. Woelfel, professor of accountancy, Southern Illinois University, Carbondale, Illinois.

7. Marketing Methods

1. Many concepts outlined in this chapter were obtained from ideas found in *Guerrilla Marketing: Secrets for Making Big Profits from Your Small Business*, by Jay Conrad Levinson (Houghton Mifflin Company, Boston, 1984); and *Streetfighting: Low-Cost Advertising/Promotion Strategies for Your Small Business*, by Jeff Slutsky with Woody Woodruff (Prentice Hall, Englewood Cliffs, New Jersey, 1984).

8. The Marketing Plan—Core of the Business Plan

1. This chapter is a compendium of information contained in the following Small Business Administration Management Aids:

- MA 2.022: *Business Plan for Small Service Firms*, by Staff Members, Education Division, Office of Management Assistance, U.S. Small Business Administration.
- MA 4.002: *Creative Selling: The Competitive Edge*, by William H. Bolen, professor and head, Department of Marketing, Georgia Southern College, Statesboro, Georgia.
- MA 4.012: *Marketing Checklist for Small Retailers*, by Michael W. Little, assistant professor of marketing, School of Business, Virginia Commonwealth University, Richmond, Virginia.
- MA 4.015: *Advertising Guidelines for Small Retail Firms*, by Ovid Riso, former vice president, Philco Ford International.
- MA 4.018: *Plan Your Advertising Budget*, by Steuart Henderson Britt, Chairman, Britt and Frerichs, Inc., Chicago, Illinois.
- MA 4.019: *Learning about Your Market*, by J. Ford Laumer, Jr., James R. Harris, and Hugh J. Guffey, Jr., assistant professors of marketing, Auburn University, Auburn, Alabama.

The chapter also incorporates ideas gleaned from the following books: *Guerrilla Marketing: Secrets for Making Big Profits from Your Small Business*, by Jay Conrad Levinson (Houghton Mifflin Company, Boston, 1984). *Streetfighting: Low-Cost Advertising/Promotion Strategies for Your Small Business*, by Jeff Slutsky with Woody Woodruff (Prentice Hall, Englewood Cliffs, New Jersey, 1984).

2. MA 4.019: *Learning About Your Market.*

3. Information on preparation of a marketing budget was compiled from MA 4.018: *Plan Your Advertising Budget.*

4. At press time, a management consulting firm called The Human Resources Group (HRG) had announced that it would review business plans. HRG's address is P.O. Box 8441, Rolling Meadows, Illinois 60008.

9. Liability

1. Attorney Barry M. Snyder's booklet, *The Captain and the Law*, is a major source of information for this chapter. The booklet is available to those who attend his classes on the subject. Contact Barry M. Snyder, P.A., Attorney at Law, 2020 NE 163rd Street, Suite 300, North Miami Beach, Florida 33162.

2. *McAllister v. Magnolia Petroleum Co.*, 357 U.S. 221 (1958), 78 S. Ct. 1201, 2 L.Ed.2d 1272.

3. Section 33 of the Merchant Marine Act of 1920, codified as 46 U.S.C. § 688 (1920).

4. 46 U.S.C. § 688 (1920), with amendments.

5. *The Osceola*, 189 U.S. 158, 159, 23 S.Ct. 483, 47 L.Ed. 760 (1903); *Mahnich v. Southern Steamship Co.*, 321 U.S. 96, 64 S.Ct. 455, 88 L.Ed. 561 (1944), et al.

6. *Koistinen v. American Export Lines, Inc.*, 83 N.Y.S.2d 297 (N.Y. City Ct. 1948).

7. *Kermarec v. Transatlantique*, 358 U.S. 625, 79 S.Ct. 406, 3 L.Ed.2d 550 (1959), et al.

8. *Moore v. American Scantic Line, Inc.*, 121 F.2d 767 (2d Cir. 1941).

9. 46 U.S.C. §§ 761-768 (1920).

10. 49 U.S.C. §§ 781, 782 (1950).

11. 33 U.S.C. §§ 1251-1376 (1972). Subsequent references in the text to "the act" are to this citation.

12. 40 CFR § 110.3(b) (1988).

13. 40 CFR § 110 (1988) and 33 CFR §§ 153.201- 205 (1988); 33 U.S.C. § 1321(b)(5) (1972) and 33 CFR § 153.205 (1988).

14. See the Federal Maritime Lien Act, 46 U.S.C. §§ 911-984 (1920), also known as the Ship Mortgage Act, 1920.

15. *Pierside Terminal Operators, Inc. v. M/V Floridian*, 389 F.Supp. 25 (E.D. Va. 1974).

16. 6 U.S.C. § 971 (1920).

17. 46 U.S.C. § 181 (1851).

10. Boat Licenses

1. This chapter relies on 46 CFR Subchapter G: *Documentation and Measurement of Vessels*. It is found in 46 CFR Parts 41-69: *Load Lines, Documentation, Admeasurement*. (See Appendix G for ordering instructions from Government Printing Office.)

2. Coast Guard Consumer Fact Sheet #8, June 1984.

3. 46 CFR 67.45-3.

4. 46 CFR 67.17-3 through 67.17-11.

5. 46 CFR Part 69.

6. 46 CFR 67.01-5.

7. Summarized from 33 CFR 2.05-25.

8. Summarized from 46 CFR Subpart 67.15: *Marking Requirements for Vessel Documentation*.

9. Summarized from 46 CFR Subpart 67.43: *Fees*.

11. Inspected Vessels—What Makes Them Different?

1. 46 CFR § 166-199, Subchapter S: *Subdivision and Stability Requirements for All Inspected Vessels;* and Subchapter T: *Small Passenger Vessels* (under 100 Gross Tons).

2. 46 CFR, Subchapter T.

3. 46 CFR 176.01-5

4. 46 CFR 176.01-40

5. 46 CFR §§ 1-40: *Safety, Boarding, Licensing, Manning—Uninspected Vessels, Tank Vessels*.

12. Captain's Licenses and Endorsements

1. Navigable waters are outlined in 33 CFR § 2.05-25, and are discussed in the chapter on boat licenses.

2. 46 CFR § 24.10-3; and 46 CFR § 175.10-28.

3. A major reorganization of the Coast Guard licensing structure (46 CFR Parts 10 and 15) was promulgated by an Interim Final Rule effective December 1, 1987, and amended by a Final Rule effective February 3, 1989. The remainder of this chapter includes changes made by that reorganization. An excellent reference on the entire Coast Guard licensing system is *U.S. Coast Guard Licenses and Certificates*, by Gregory D. Szczurek (Azure Communications, P.O. Box 23387, New Orleans, Louisiana, 70183-0387; updated 1989).

The extensive changes to 46 CFR Parts 10 and 15 made it necessary to cut and paste many notes from the Federal Register to keep them usable. The Government Printing Office is not expected to reissue Parts 10 and 15 until 1991. During the interim, readers unable to find an accurate cut-and-paste copy might contact Houston Marine Training Services at 800-535-8803 for a nominally priced, computer-generated copy that is complete as of February 3, 1989.

4. Mandated by 46 CFR § 10.103. Boundary lines are described in 46 CFR Part 7. (See Appendix C for extract.)

5. 46 CFR § 10.103.

6. 46 CFR § Parts 10 and 15.

7. 46 CFR § 10.103.

8. 46 CFR § 10.466.

9. 46 CFR § Parts 10 and 15.

10. 46 CFR § 24.10-23; and 46 CFR § 175.10-27.

11. 46 CFR § 175.10-27(b)(6).

12. Houston Marine Training Services, a division of EXAMCO, Inc., 1600 20th Street, Kenner, Louisiana 70062.

13. The references are 46 CFR § 10.429 and 46 CFR § 10.456 for limited masters; 46 CFR § 10.466 for limited six-packs.

14. From a paper by Paul Raymond Von Protz, "A View From Under," September 20, 1987.

15. 46 CFR § 10.209.

13. Administrative Law—He Who Giveth Can Taketh Away

1. This chapter draws upon information contained in 46 CFR Part 4, *Marine Casualties and Investigations*; and Part 5, *Marine Investigation Regulations—Personnel Action*.

2. 46 CFR § 4.07-5 requires "persons having knowledge of the subject matter of the investigation to answer questionnaires" and to produce "relevant books, papers, documents and other records." Lieutenant Commander J. Pierce Guyer, an investigating officer, explains that failure to do so may result in a charge of misconduct against the license holder.

3. 46 CFR § 5.105.

4. Ibid. 5.23; see 46 CFR § 5.27, 5.29, 5.31, 5.33, and 5.57, respectively.

5. Information concerning administrative law judges was derived from 46 CFR § 5.19, and from an interview with John Jordan, legal assistant to the chief judge, Coast Guard Headquarters, Washington, D.C.

6. Information for the sections on prehearing, hearing, reopening, and appeals was taken from 46 CFR Subparts 5.5, 5.6, and 5.7, respectively.

7. 46 CFR § 5.61.

8. Ibid. 5.59.

9. Ibid. Subpart 5.9.

10. John Jordan, legal assistant to the chief judge.

14. Bareboat Chartering for Pleasure

1. *Bareboat Demise Charter Guidelines—The Coast Guard View* (see Appendix B); extracted from U.S. Coast Guard COMDTINST M16000.7; 10.A.4.f.

2. USCG COMDTINST M16000.7; 10.A.4.c.

3. Ibid. 10.A.4.f.

4. Ibid. 10.A.4.e.

5. Ibid.

6. Section 33, Merchant Marine Act of 1920, codified as 46 U.S.C. 688.

15. The Captain's Responsibilities

1. David W. Bethany, Captain, *Misty*, P.O. Box 1108, Inglis, Florida 32649; observed by the author, who was mate.

2. National Captain's Institute, P.O. Box 13714, St. Petersburg, Florida 33733, prepares a kit containing a notary commission, seal, stamp, and four-year bond for captains intending to perform weddings in Florida waters. Cost at press time was $79.

3. Excerpted and summarized from an article by the author for American Professional Captains Association, July 1986, P.O. Box 350398, Fort Lauderdale, Florida 33316. The dive-boat skipper's name is omitted purposely to avoid unnecessary embarrassment related to a case that is now closed. It is a matter of record in U.S. Coast Guard Docket no. 07-0016-MEH-85, Case no. 16722.06.

Bibliography

Code of Federal Regulations (Titles 33 and 46). Washington, D.C.: Government Printing Office.

Defense Mapping Agency Hydrographic/Topographic Center. *American Practical Navigator.* 2 vols. Washington, D.C., 1977.

———. *Chart No. 1.*

———. *List of Lights Including Fog Signals: . . .* [East and West] Coasts of North and South America ... (Pubs 110 and 111).

———. *Radio Navigational Aids . . .* (Pubs 117-A and 117-B).

———. *Sailing Directions.*

Eagleson, Jane. "Liveaboard Charter Operators Blend Business With Pleasure." *Soundings,* October 1987.

Flannery, Jim. "Developer Gambling on Turning Oil Rigs Into Floating Casinos." *Soundings,* October 1987.

Internal Revenue Service. *Information for Business Taxpayers.* Publication 583 (1988).

———. *Tax Guide for Small Businesses.* Publication 334 (1988).

———. *Tax Information on Corporations.* Publication 542 (1986).

Kotsch, William J. *Weather for the Mariner.* Annapolis, Md.: Naval Institute Press, 1983.

Levinson, Jay Conrad. *Guerrilla Marketing: Secrets for Making Big Profits from Your Small Business.* Boston: Houghton Mifflin Company, 1984.

Light List. Washington, D.C.: Government Printing Office.

Maloney, Elbert S. *Chapman Piloting, Seamanship & Small Boat Handling.* 56th ed. New York: Hearst Books, 1983.

———. *Dutton's Navigation & Piloting.* 13th ed. Annapolis, Md.: Naval Institute Press, 1978.

Maritime Administration. *Marine Fire Prevention, Firefighting and Fire Safety.* Washington, D.C.

National Ocean Service. *Coast Pilot,* Atlantic, Gulf, and Pacific Coasts; Atlantic and Gulf Intracoastal Waterways; the Great Lakes. Rockville, Md.

———. *Tide Tables, Current Tables,* and *Tidal Current Charts.*

The Ship's Medicine Chest and First Aid at Sea. Government Printing Office, Washington, D.C.

Slutsky, Jeff, with Woody Woodruff. *Streetfighting: Low-Cost Advertising/Promotion Strategies for Your Small Business.* Englewood Cliffs, N.J.: Prentice Hall, 1984.

Small Business Administration. *A Venture Capital Primer for Small Business.* SBA MA 1.009.

———. *The ABC's of Borrowing.* SBA MA 1.001.

———. *Accounting Services for Small Service Firms.* SBA MA 1.010.

———. *Advertising Guidelines for Small Retail Firms.* SBA MA 4.015.

———. *Analyze Your Records to Reduce Costs.* SBA MA 1.011.

———. *Basic Budgets for Profit Planning.* SBA MA 1.004.

———. *Budgeting in a Small Service Firm.* SBA MA 1.015.

———. *Business Plan for Retailers.* SBA MA 2.020.

———. *Business Plan for Small Service Firms.* SBA MA 2.022.

———. *Checklist for Going into Business.* SBA MA 2.016.

———. *Creative Selling: The Competitive Edge.* SBA MA 4.002.

———. *Learning about Your Market.* SBA MA 4.019.

———. *Marketing Checklist for Small Retailers.* SBA MA 4.012.

———. *Plan Your Advertising Budget.* SBA MA 4.018.

———. *Sound Cash Management and Borrowing.* SBA MA 1.016.

———. *Thinking about Going into Business?* SBA MA 2.025.

Snyder, Barry M. *The Captain and the Law.* Self published. 2020 NE 163rd Street, Suite 300, North Miami Beach, FL 33162.

Stapleton, Sid. "Say Goodby to the Office." *Motor Boating & Sailing,* May 1987.

Szczurek, Gregory D. *U.S. Coast Guard Licenses and Certificates.* Updated February 3, 1989. New Orleans: Azure Communications, 1988.

U.S. Coast Guard. *Boating Safety Training Manual* (COMDTINST M16759.4b). Office of Boating, Public, and Consumer Affairs, Washington, D.C.

———. "Documenting Your Boat: Pros and Cons." Consumer Fact Sheet #8 (June 1984). Office of Boating, Public, and Consumer Affairs, Washington, D.C.

————. "IALA Buoyage System Pamphlet" (ANSC SN 3022). Commandant (G-NSR-1), Washington, D.C.

————. "Marine Aids to Navigation." (CG-193). Commandant (G-NSR), Washington, D.C.

————. *Navigation Rules, International-Inland.* (COMDTINST M16672.2A). Washington, D.C.: Government Printing Office, 1983.

Watchkeeping for Seafarers (Basic Principles to be Observed in Keeping a Navigational/Engineering Watch), 1978.

Index